A PLACE FOR WE

by Archie Maddocks

‖SAMUEL FRENCH‖

A NOTE FROM THE DIRECTOR

I first came across *A Place for We* as part of Talawa Firsts, our new writing festival, which has proved to be a great platform for some of the most exciting Black writers in the country. We knew there was something special about *A Place for We*, and indeed about Archie as a writer. The story is humorous but also has great depth and is so layered that the simplest questions asked by a character provide a springboard for myriad thoughts and even more questions about the places we call home, and about identity and belonging.

As I look at the brick work here at Park Theatre, I realise that this place also contains the essence of this play within its structure; the history and stories witnessed by these walls. The movement of the people through this area, each trying to make a living for themselves and their families, battling with life and all it throws at them. The bricks remain the same, so it seems do the aims of the people within the walls. Each outgoing occupant sees the incoming as different, threatening, yet their wants and needs are so similar as to be comical.

This does not pardon the injustice of gentrification. The injustice is common to all no matter who is carrying out the gentrification; cheap property is lost at the expense of one community or another, the incoming culture replaces that of the outgoing communities. Whether a coffee shop replaces a grocer specialising in traditional fruit and vegetables, there are winners and losers in this scenario. It is a difficult and ongoing conundrum.

It is great to be back in a theatre, at Park Theatre especially, a space where we can laugh and cry together as we grapple with the difficult questions posed by this most enthralling writer.

Michael Buffong, Director
Artistic Director, Talawa Theatre

USE OF COPYRIGHTED MUSIC

A licence issued by Concord Theatricals to perform this play does
not include permission to use the incidental music specified in this
publication. In the United Kingdom: Where the place of performance
is already licensed by the PERFORMING RIGHT SOCIETY (PRS)
a return of the music used must be made to them. If the place of
performance is not so licensed then application should be made to PRS
for Music (www.prsformusic.com.). A separate and additional licence
from PHONOGRAPHIC PERFORMANCE LTD.(www. ppluk.com) may
be needed whenever commercial recordings are used. Outside the United
Kingdom: Please contact the appropriate music licensing authority in
your territory for the rights to any incidental music.

USE OF COPYRIGHTED THIRD-PARTY MATERIALS

Licensees are solely responsible for obtaining formal written permission
from copyright owners to use copyrighted third-party materials (e.g.,
artworks, logos) in the performance of this play and are strongly cautioned
to do so. If no such permission is obtained by the licensee, then the
licensee must use only original materials that the licensee owns and
controls. Licensees are solely responsible and liable for clearances of all
third-party copyrighted materials, and shall indemnify the copyright
owners of the play(s) and their licensing agent, Concord Theatricals Ltd.,
against any costs, expenses, losses and liabilities arising from the use of
such copyrighted third-party materials by licensees.

IMPORTANT BILLING AND CREDIT REQUIREMENTS

If you have obtained performance rights to this title, please refer to your
licensing agreement for important billing and credit requirements.

FOR AMATEUR PRODUCTION ENQUIRIES

UNITED KINGDOM AND WORLD
EXCLUDING NORTH AMERICA
licensing@concordtheatricals.co.uk
020-7054-7298

Each title is subject to availability from Concord Theatricals, depending upon country of performance.

A NOTE FROM THE WRITER

Things *always* change.

That's the nature of society. It's what we, as humans, do. It's in our nature as a species to constantly move, shift, innovate, adapt. That's why we have created what we have and live in the places we do. It's how we got out of the food chain (thank god for that!).

However, change is not readily accepted by those that it is negatively affecting. Why would it be? It means having to adapt to something you don't understand, when in essence, that very changeability is threatening your existence. Why would you welcome that? It's a perfectly understandable reaction to grasp. We have a tendency to want to reject change. It's represents the unknown and for most, the unknown is a terrifying concept – one which almost always leads someone to assume that the worst is going to happen.

With *A Place for We*, I wanted to look at the nature of change and how it affects the people that it happens to. More specifically, I wanted to look at how the ever changing demographic of both people and money may affect an ever evolving area and a constantly reinventing community. The term now is gentrification. However, that kind of shift, new people moving in and old people moving out, has always happened, particularly in cities. Where gentrification as a concept is flawed is the speed at which it happens, it's so rapid that it doesn't allow for people to adapt, which can (in my opinion) lead to the erosion of community... as we knew it anyway.

With more money comes the ability to change things more quickly. And with that speed, that's where things (and people) become lost in the ever-swelling sea of development.

This play came from a moment when I was about 22 or so. I was working at an undertakers' at the time so was fully immersed in that world. One day, I was walking to Brixton Village, I had a friend that worked in there. Walking through Brixton, I saw what I had always seen when I visited the area, a vast mix but clearly defined community of people. Stepping into Brixton Village though, I saw *different* people. They were mostly white, obviously middle class and completely oblivious to the Brixton that I knew. Even more weird, I hadn't seen any of them outside of the market, so my main question was whether or not they had just teleported in. The moment has stuck with me because it was the first time I properly noticed gentrification like that. I'd seen Hackney fall, and been in and around Portobello when things started to become more upmarket. However, I had never seen the shift happen so quickly. And it made me wonder what happens to those people that either can't, or won't change? Do they just get left behind? Does everything that they had just disappear? And, more importantly, does anyone remember them or care about what they left behind?

It's a question I still ask today as someone who both benefits from encroaching gentrification (used to only go to Hackney to get shot at, now it's where I get my vegan chicken) and laments its ravenous appetite.

I'd always been fascinated by the things we let go and the things we keep. Additionally, I've always been interested by the things we keep up, just because it's what we always do. That's partly what this play aims to discuss. The little traditions that we keep up, even if we don't fully understand them. When it comes down to it, the question I ask myself is who are those traditions for, and why do they keep them going if we don't fully understand what they are?

I think that they're for the people that came before us and keeping them going is our unwitting way of honouring them. So even though we don't remember, in a weird way, they aren't forgotten.

Archie Maddocks

The World Premiere of *A Place for We* took place at Park Theatre, London (Artistic Director Jez Bond; Executive Director Rachael Williams) on 7 Oct 2021 as a co-production with Talawa Theatre Company (Artistic Director Michael Buffong; Executive Director Carolyn ML Forsyth) with the following team:

CAST

Young Clarence James *Harold Addo*
George O'Driscoll / Austin / Angus *Blake Harrison*
Anna O'Driscoll / Violet *Joanna Horton*
Tasha / Esme *Kirsty Oswald*
Keron James *Laurence Ubong Williams*
Clarence James / Elmorn James *David Webber*

CREATIVE TEAM

Writer *Archie Maddocks*
Director *Michael Buffong*
Set & Costume Designer *Louie Whitemore*
Lighting Designer *Sherry Coenen*
Sound Designer *Tony Gayle*
Dialect Coach *Hazel Holder*
Associate Sound Designer *Bella Kear*
Assistant Director *Lo Feliciani Ojeda*
Production Manager *Jerome Reid*
Production Electrician & Programmer *Jake Lawrence*
Costume Supervisor *Claire Nicolas*
Costume Assistant *András Jacobs*

Producer *Daniel Cooper*
Company Stage Manager *Kala Simpson*
Assistant Stage Manager *Emily Mei Ling Pearce*
Stage Management Intern *Tayla Hunter*

CAST

Harold Addo | Young Clarence James

Harold Addo trained at East 15 Acting School.

Theatre includes: *Holes* (Nottingham Playhouse/UK Tour); *Sing Yer Heart Out For The Lads* (Chichester Festival Theatre); *Spring Awakening* (Young Vic); *Billy Budd* (Royal Opera House); *Hamlet, Treasure Island* (Iris Theatre); *Womb* (Bush Theatre); *The Gift of the Gab* (White Bear Theatre); *Beyond the Blue* (Theatre Royal Stratford East); *Waiting For Godot* (Sweaty Palms production/site specific); *It Might Never Happen* (Doll's Eye Theatre/ UK Tour); *Ella Enchanted* (Edinburgh Fringe); *The 49* (Theatre N16); *Cloud Tectonics, Jesus Hopped the 'A' Train* (Corbett Theatre); *4.48 Psychosis* (Etcetera Theatre); and *Liliom: A Legend in Seven Scenes* (Bread and Roses).

Television includes: *Psyched!, Locked Up Abroad/Banged Up Abroad* and *PREMature*.

Film includes: *PhatNav* and *Beatrice*.

Blake Harrison | George O'Driscoll / Austin / Angus

For Park Theatre: *End of the Pier.*

Theatre includes: *Waitress* (Adelphi Theatre, West End); *Step 9 (of 12)* (Trafalgar Studios); *The Accidental Lives of Memorise* (Not/Applicable Theatre).

Television includes: *The Great, Dr. Who, World on Fire, A Very English Scandal, Jack & the Beanstalk: After Ever After, Kate & Koji, Agatha and the Midnight Murders, Death in Paradise, Agatha and the Truth of Murder, Trust Me, Prime Suspect – 1973, Houdini and Doyle, The Increasingly Poor Decisions of Todd Margaret* (Series 1, 2 & 3), *Edge of Heaven, Tripped, Big Bad World, Way To Go, The Bleak Old Shop of Stuff, Them From That Thing, Him and Her* (Series 1 & 2), *White Van Man* (2 Series), *The Inbetweeners* (3 series), *The Bill.*

Film includes: *The Kindred, Hooves of Clay* (starred in and directed), *Madness in the Method, Dad's Army, Game Over, Inbetweeners 2, Keeping Rosy, Inbetweeners: The Movie, The Tin Snail, Reuniting the Rubins.*

Joanna Horton | Anna O'Driscoll / Violet

Theatre includes: *Blank* (Donmar Warehouse); *Othello* (Shakespeare's Globe); *All's Well That Ends Well, As You Like It, The Gods Weep, Days Of Significance* (RSC); *Belongings* (Hampstead Theatre); *The Cherry Orchard* (Birmingham Rep); *Town* (Royal & Derngate); *Once A Catholic* (Royal Court).

Television includes: *Professor T, Endeavour, Dark Angel, The People Next Door, Silent Witness, Partners In Crime, Knifeman, The Suspicions Of Mr Whicher, Father Brown, London's Burning, Doctors, Permanently Excluded, Holby City, New Tricks, The Bill, Breaking The Mould, Midnight Man, Bike Squad, Holby Blue, Five Days, Robin Hood, Spooks, Eleventh Hour, Afterlife, Foyle's War.*

Film includes: *Fish Tank, The Listener.*

Radio includes: *Barnaby Rudge, Sandman of the Gulf.*

Kirsty Oswald | Tasha / Esme

Theatre includes: *The Girl on the Train* (West End & UK Tour); *Uncle Vanya* (Hampstead Theatre); *Things I Know To Be True, Othello* (Frantic Assembly); *The Father* (Theatre Royal Bath/West End); *We Are Proud To Present...* (Bush Theatre); *The Winter's Tale* (Sheffield Crucible); *The Judas Kiss* (Hampstead/UK Tour/West End).

Television includes: *Endeavour, The Coroner, Beowulf, Salting The Battlefield, Ripper Street, Holby City, Doctors, Dancing on the Edge,* and *Sadie J.*

Film includes: *Gutterdammerung, A Little Chaos,* and *Le Weekend.*

Radio includes: *Jude the Obscure, Hi Spec, The Tzars, Lifelines, Moll Flanders, Charles Paris, Blake in Lambeth, The Beaten Track* and *The Gifts of War.*

Kirsty trained at Rose Bruford and won the Highly Commended Award at the Spotlight Prize and was runner up for the Carleton Hobbs Award.

Laurence Ubong Williams | Keron James

Theatre includes: *The Welkin* (National Theatre); *The Deep Blue Sea* (Chichester Festival Theatre); *The Glass Piano* (The Print Room @ Coronet); *The Watsons* (Chichester Festival Theatre); *Top Trumps* (Theatre503); *Jumpy* (Theatr Clwyd); *The Winter's Tale* (Orange Tree Theatre); *How To Find Us* (Soho Theatre); *Othello: Deconstructed* (Oxford School Of Drama - The North Wall).

Television includes: *The Capture, Back, Humans, Doctors.*

Film includes: *My Dinner With Herve.*

David Webber | Clarence James / Elmorn James

Theatre includes: *2020 Collection: 'A New America'* (Tara Arts Theatre); *Wonderful Storybook* (Theatre Peckham); *The High Table* (The Bush, London/ The Rep, Birmingham); *Barber Shop Chronicles* (National Theatre); *Arms And The Man* (Watford Palace Theatre); *The Hudsucker Proxy* (Nuffield Southampton & Liverpool Playhouse); *When Blair Had Bush & Bunga* (Lee Menzies Productions); *Catch-22* (Northern Stage); *Sweet and Bird of Youth* (Old Vic); *The Government Inspector* (Young Vic); *Twelfth Night* (Nottingham Playhouse); *Death and The King's Horseman* (National Theatre); *The Wizard of Oz* (Theatre Royal, Northampton); *Aladdin* (Watford Palace); *The Big Life* (Bill Kenwright/Apollo, Shaftesbury Avenue); *What's In The Cat* (Contact Theatre, Manchester/Royal Court, London); *Master Harold & The Boys* (Southwark Playhouse); *Othello, The Sneeze* (Good Company); *The Bassett Table* (Bristol Old Vic/Wild Iris); *The Wizard of Oz* (New Vic Theatre, Stoke-on-Trent); *Night and Day* (Northampton Theatre Royal); *Flyin' West, The Looking Glass, King Lear, The Lion, Smile Orange, The Road* (Talawa Theatre); *The Beatification of Area Boy* (West Yorkshire Playhouse); *Downfall* (Manchester Court); *Leave Taking* (National Theatre); *Merchant of Venice* (Manchester Library Theatre); *Antony and Cleopatra* (Talawa Theatre/Liverpool Everyman); *Hiawatha* (Bristol Old Vic); *No One Writes to the Colonel* (Hammersmith Lyric Theatre); *Ragamuffin, The Colored Museum* (Double Edge); *Remembrance* (Tricycle Theatre / Carib).

Television includes: *Half Bad, Death in Paradise, Year of the Rabbit, The Educatoror, Chewing Gum, Holby City, Youngers* (Series 2), *Nan, The Royal Bodyguard, How Not To Live Your Life, Sarah Jane Adventures, Being Human, No Heroics, The Afternoon Play - Pieces of a Silver Lining, Doctors, Funland, The Taming of The Shrew, EastEnders, Grass, London's Burning, Homie & Away, The Knock, Accused, Prime Suspect TV, 2 Point 4 Children, Coronation Street, The Bill, Brittas Empire.*

Film includes: *The Children Act, Captain Phillips, Broken, Mrs. Palfrey at the Claremont, London Voodoo, All Or Nothing, 51st State, Among Giants, The Avengers, Getting Hurt.*

Radio includes: *Forty-Three-Fifty-Nine-Wake, Blues for Mr. Charlie, Lunch Hour Rush.*

CREATIVE TEAM

Archie Maddocks | Writer

Archie is a multi-award winning/nominated writer and stand up comedian. As a writer, he's had work produced at the Bush Theatre, Lyric Hammersmith, Orange Tree Theatre, Royal Court, and in New York at the New Light Theatre, has had two plays produced for BBC Radio 4 and has several projects in active development for TV and Film. He's been a part of the BBC Writersroom *London Voices* and in 2018 he was selected as part of the prestigious 4Screenwriting course. He was also the Writer in Residence at BBC Radio Drama.

A Place for We was shortlisted for the Bruntwood Prize and the Alfred Fagon Award.

As a stand up comedian, he's worked in the biggest clubs in the UK, and as far afield as South Africa and the USA. He's taken four solo shows to the Edinburgh Fringe, which have all garnered 4 and 5 star reviews and has transferred the last three shows to Soho Theatre. Two of his shows can be viewed on NextUp.com, an online platform exclusively for stand up comedy.

Represented by Alec Drysdale at Independent Talent Group.

Michael Buffong | Director

Michael is the Artistic Director of Talawa Theatre Company. He has previously directed: *Private Lives, All the Ordinary Angels, Six Degrees of Separation, On My Birthday* and the multi-award winning *A Raisin in the Sun* for the Royal Exchange Theatre. Most recently he has directed *Guys & Dolls, King Lear, All My Sons* (Talawa Theatre Company and Royal Exchange Theatre), and *A Kind of People* (Royal Court.)

Louie Whitemore | Set & Costume Designer

Offie Nominated for Best Costume Designer for *The Daughter-in-Law* (Arcola Theatre), Best Set Designer for *Tonight at 8.30* and ONCOMM winner for *15 Heroines* (Jermyn Street). OldVic12 2016 finalist, JMK 2010 Finalist. Associate Designer to Jermyn Street Theatre.

For Park Theatre: *The Last Temptation of Boris Johnson.*

Theatre includes: *Krapp's Last Tape / Eh Joe / Old Tune* (Jermyn Street Theatre); *Stewart Lee: Content Provider / Snowflake / Tornado* (UK Tour and BBC 2); *Potted Sherlock* (Vaudeville Theatre, UK Tour); *Three Birds* (Bush Theatre/Royal Exchange Manchester); *Good Soul* (Young Vic); *Egusi Soup* (Soho Theatre); *Mud* (Gate Theatre); *The Daughter-In-Law, The Dog, the Night and the Knife, A Game of Love and Chance* (Arcola Theatre); *Handbagged, Single Spies, Bold Girls, Miss Julie, Creditors, Lady Killers, Little Voice, Dear Uncle* (Theatre by the Lake); *Stage in the Park* (Watford); *Blithe Spirit* (Beijing); *Original Death Rabbit, Footprints Festival, For Services Rendered, Tonight At 8.30,*

Tomorrow At Noon, Creditors, Miss Julie (Jermyn Street Theatre); *The Minotaur, My Father Odysseus* (Unicorn Theatre); *The Winter's Tale* (NAPA Karachi); *Lost Land* (Jenin, Palestine); *Shakespeare Untold, The Magic Playroom* (UK Tour, Pleasance Theatre); *I Am A Superhero* (Old Vic New Voices at Theatre503); *Buttons* (King's Head, Islington).

Opera includes: *Messiah* (Danish Opera, Frankfurt Opera); *Carmen* (Dorset Opera); *Banished* (Blackheath Halls); *Serse / Der Kaiser* (RSC Glasgow); *Opera Makers* (GSMD); *ETO Autumn Scenes 2020* (UK Tour); *The Magic Flute, Carmen, La Bohème, Albert Herring, The Marriage of Figaro* (costume design for Co Opera Co).

Dance includes: *Nora / She Persisted* (English National Ballet); *The Nutcracker* (Shanghai Ballet); *Egle* (Lithuania National Ballet); *ENB Choreographics Programme 2015 - 2017, Dance Journeys 2016/2017/ 2019/2020* (English National Ballet at Sadler's Wells/The Barbican).

Louie is also a founding member of The Freelance Network and the Set and Costume Designer representative for the Director Designer Equity Committee.

Sherry Coenen | Lighting Designer

Sherry has been lighting shows in the US and UK since graduating with a BFA in Lighting Design from the University of Miami.

For Park Theatre: *Skin Tight, Chicken Soup, Crystal Springs, Much Ado About Nothing, Happy to Help.*

Credits include: *Operation Mincemeat* (NDT KOI nominated 2019); *Frankenstein* (BAC KOI winner 2019); *The Singing Mermaid* (Little Angel Theatre); *Izindava* (UK Tour); *This is How We Die* (UK Tour); *Cinderella* (Queen's Theatre Hornchurch); *CELL* (UK Tour); *Conquest of the South Pole, These Trees are Made of Blood* (Arcola); *Brrr!* (UK Tour); *5 Guys Chillin'* (Kings Head); *Anton Chekhov* (Hampstead Theatre).

Tony Gayle | Sound Designer

Sound Design includes: *Get Up, Stand Up! The Bob Marley Musical* (Lyric); *Gin Craze!* (Royal & Derngate); *And Breathe* (Almeida); *Shoe Lady* (Royal Court); *Poet In da Corner* (Almeida & UK Tour); *Beautiful: The Carole King Musical* (UK Tour); *Dirty Rotten Scoundrels* (Bernie Grants Arts Centre); *Songs For Nobodies* (Ambassadors); *The Wild Party* (The Other Palace); *Lazarus* (Kings Cross); *Candide* (Bridewell); *Floyd Collins* (Wiltons Hall).

Associate Sound Design includes: *Dear Evan Hansen* (Noel Coward); *TINA* (Worldwide); *Jersey Boys* (London & UK Tour); *Groundhog Day* (Old Vic); Disney's *Aladdin* (Prince Edward and Europe); *Beautiful: The Carole King Musical* (Aldwych); *Here Lies Love* (National Theatre and Seattle Rep); *Saturday Night Fever* (UK Tour); *The Book of Mormon* (Prince of Wales); *Spring Awakening* (Novello).

Hazel Holder | Dialect Coach

Hazel Holder has been an actor, singer and theatre maker for over thirty years and then retrained gaining her MA in Voice Studies at Royal Central School of Speech and Drama. Hazel has worked with pioneering companies such as Clod Ensemble as a Performing Medicine Associate Artist, MonoBox, Clean Break, Marginal Voices (working with trafficked women), and Cast Women's Charity - 'helping to transform vulnerable women's lives through creative holistic education'.

Theatre includes: *Rockets & Blue Lights, Death of England: Delroy, Death of England, Small Island, Nine Night, Barber Shop Chronicles, Pericles, Angels in America, Les Blancs* and *Ma Rainey's Black Bottom* (National Theatre); *Constellations* (Donmar at the Vaudeville); *2:22* (The Noel Coward Theatre); *Death of a Black Man* (Hampstead Theatre); *Uncle Vanya* (Harold Pinter); *Pass Over* (Kiln Theatre); *Death of a Salesman* (Piccadilly Theatre / Young Vic); *Caroline, or Change* (Chichester Festival Theatre at The Playhouse Theatre, Hampstead Theatre and Chichester); *Fairview, The Convert, The Mountaintop, The Emperor* (Young Vic); *Cuttin' It* (Young Vic / Royal Court); *Dreamgirls* (Resident Director at The Savoy); *Guys and Dolls and Girls* (Talawa Theatre and at the Royal Exchange, also at Soho Theatre); *The Goat, or Who is Sylvia?* (Theatre Royal Haymarket); *Ear for Eye, Poet in Da Corner, Grimly Handsome, Pigs & Dogs, Father Comes Home from the Wars* (Royal Court).

Television includes: As voice/dialect coach: *Small Axe* (Steve McQueen Anthology); *The Power, In the Long Run* (Jimmy Akingbola).

Film includes: *The Silent Twins*; *Death on the Nile* (Letitia Wright).

As a performer, theatre credits include: *Here We Go, As You Like It, Medea,* and *Death and the King's Horseman* (National Theatre); *The Bakkhai* (Almeida); *The Tempest* (RSC); *The Bacchae* (National Theatre of Scotland/Lincoln Center, Broadway); *The Sleeping Beauty* (Young Vic, Barbican, New Victory, Broadway).

Bella Kear | Associate Sound Designer

Bella is a London based sound designer from Hertfordshire. She is a 2021 graduate from LAMDA where her credits included; *Antipodes, Love and Information,* and *The Spalding Suite.* Her designs typically revolve around her love of music and film scores, and her study of psychoacoustics. As a student she also worked as a sound editor and has an interest in binaural sound and Foley. Her most recent credit was *Flux* at Theatre 503.

Lo Feliciani Ojeda | Assistant Director

Lo Feliciani Ojeda is an actor, director, and deviser from Caracas, Venezuela. They are a current MFA candidate at East 15 Acting School, and a 2020 graduate at the University of North Carolina School of the Arts.

Directing credits include: *The Odyssey, Dry Land, Antigone, Platform 2* (East 15).

Daniel Cooper | Producer

Daniel Cooper is the Producer Programmer of Park Theatre.

For Park Theatre: *Park Bench* (an original concept for a digital-come-live theatre play) and assistant producer on *Ian McKellen with Shakespeare, Tolkien, Others & You, End of the Pier, The Other Place, Rosenbaum's Rescue, Whodunnit [Unrehearsed], The Weatherman, Sydney & the Old Girl* (with Miram Margolyes), *La Cage aux Folles [The Play]*.

Daniel joined Park Theatre in 2017 after achieving an MA in Creative Producing (First with Distinction) from Mountview. This followed a 6-year career as a secondary school languages teacher and pastoral leader. Daniel is also a trustee of the Cervantes Theatre / Spanish Theatre Company.

ABOUT PARK THEATRE

Park Theatre was founded by Artistic Director, Jez Bond and Creative Director Emeritus, Melli Marie. The building opened in May 2013 and, with eight West End transfers, two National Theatre transfers and 25 national tours in its first eight years, quickly garnered a reputation as a key player in the London theatrical scene. Park Theatre has received five Olivier nominations, won Offie Awards for Best New Play, Best Set Design and Best Foodie Experience, and won The Stage's Fringe Theatre of the Year and Accessible Theatre Award.

Park Theatre is an inviting and accessible venue, delivering work of exceptional calibre in the heart of Finsbury Park. We work with writers, directors and designers of the highest quality to present compelling, exciting and beautifully told stories across our two intimate spaces.

Our programme encompasses a broad range of work from classics to revivals with a healthy dose of new writing, producing in-house as well as working in partnership with emerging and established producers. We strive to play our part within the UK's theatre ecology by offering mentoring, support and opportunities to artists and producers within a professional theatre-making environment.

Our Creative Learning strategy seeks to widen the number and range of people who participate in theatre, and provides opportunities for those with little or no prior contact with the arts.

In everything we do we aim to be warm and inclusive; a safe, welcoming and wonderful space in which to work, create and visit.

* * * * * "A five-star neighbourhood theatre." Independent

As a registered charity [number 1137223] with no regular public subsidy, we rely on the kind support of our donors and volunteers. To find out how you can get involved visit parktheatre.co.uk.

ABOUT TALAWA THEATRE COMPANY

Talawa Theatre Company is the most prominent Black theatre company in the UK.

Talawa's established production track record shines a spotlight on Black artists, creating theatre for diverse audiences across the country and internationally. Having mounted more than fifty productions over their 35-year history, Talawa's last co-production, *Superhoe* by Nicole Lecky, was at the Royal Court.

Other recent productions have included collaborations with the Royal Exchange; *Guys & Dolls*, *King Lear* (in association with Birmingham Repertory Theatre); and *All My Sons* (Royal Exchange Theatre, UK tour), and new work including *Girls* by Theresa Ikoko (co-produced with Soho Theatre, High Tide) and *Half Breed* by Natasha Marshall (co-produced with Soho Theatre).

Talawa actors, writers, directors and creative personnel now work in all areas of British theatre, film and television, underscoring the vital contribution of the company to the cultural life of the nation.

In 2022 Talawa Theatre Company will co-produce Sian Carter's *Running With Lions* with Lyric Theatre, in addition to a range of new and exciting work.

Talawa Theatre Company is led by Michael Buffong (Artistic Director and Joint CEO) and Carolyn ML Forsyth (Executive Director and Joint CEO).

Find out more about Talawa: talawa.com.

AUDIENCE FEEDBACK

We would love to know what you thought of A Place For We.

Your feedback is shared with our funders and helps us continue making high-quality, relevant and entertaining work.

The survey takes a minute to fill and can be accessed by scanning the QR code below.

SHINING A SPOTLIGHT
ON OUR PRODUCERS' CIRCLE

Park Theatre owes a huge debt of gratitude to Ian McKellen who, in July 2017, donated a week of his time, giving ten amazing performances to help us raise money for a Production Fund.

Ian and a passionate group of donors, committed to helping us produce plays, constitute our Producers' Circle. Together they help us bring productions to the stage, telling stories that resonate and reflect the world around us.

As we emerge from the pandemic, mounting in-house productions helps us to develop our audiences, celebrate and promote our values and provide opportunities for freelance creatives to do what they do best.

If you would like to find out more about the Producers' Circle or other ways you can support Park Theatre, please contact development@parktheatre.co.uk.

Park Keepers

Park Theatre is a registered charity and each year we have to raise money in order to continue delivering world-class productions to a wide audience, at affordable prices. One of the ways we invite support is through our Park Keepers scheme.

As a Keeper you can make a vital difference while enjoying a range of exciting benefits including priority booking, regular newsletters, complimentary tickets to preview performances and invitations to exclusive events.

For more information about Park Keepers, you can email us development@parktheatre.co.uk or visit parktheatre.co.uk/keepers.

FOR PARK THEATRE

THANK YOU

We would not be here without those of you who donated so generously to our Park Life campaign during the pandemic. Your support ensured our survival and we could not be more grateful to you.

As we recover, we need to continue fundraising, particularly as Park Theatre is a registered charity [number 1137223] that receives no regular public subsidy for core costs. We need to raise around £300,000 annually to enable us to remain a warm and welcoming venue to the 100,000+ people that come through our doors each year to inspire or be inspired.

We could not continue to operate without the support of the following people and organisations. Thank you for helping Park Theatre to reopen its doors, while remaining accessible and affordable to the widest possible audience:

Corporate Supporters:

Bud Flowers, Katten Muchin Rosenman UK LLP, Runway East, Savillls, Telford Homes

Trusts & Foundations:

Arts Council England: Cultural Recovery Funds, City Bridge Trust, Garfield Weston Foundation, Islington Council, Oak Foundation, St James's Trust Settlement, The Chapman Charitable Trust, The Maria Björnson Memorial Fund, The Mercers' Company, The Morris Charitable Trust, The National Lottery Community Fund, The Victoria Wood Foundation

Producers' Circle:

Katie Bradford, Marianne Falk, Nate Lalone, Claire & Scott Mackin, Ian McKellen, Lesley & Richard Reuben, Robert Timms, Antony Zaki

Special Project Donors:

Anon, Peter G. Forster, Deirdra Moynihan

Major Donors:

Michael & Sheila Black, Katie Bradford, Lady Brittan, Mark & Mo Constantine, Heraclis Economides, Islington Council, Ron & Karen Jacob, Three Monkies Trust

And to all of our generous Park Keepers, including:

Life Keepers:

Vicky Bond, Marianne Falk, Rachel Lewis, Dorcas Morgan, Leah Schmidt, Alex Sweet

Show Keepers:

Linda Almond, Richard Chapman, William Claxton-Smith, Wendy Edgar-Jones, Nick Frankfort, Nate Lalone, Frank McLoughlin, Nigel Pantling, Victoria Phillips, Nicholas Pryor, Ian Rogan, Robert Timms

CHARACTERS

CLARENCE JAMES –Defiant. 60s. Black.

KERON JAMES – Lost pessimist. Late 20s/early 30s. Mixed Race.

TASHA – Sharp as a tack, but has no idea – an optimist. Late 20s. White.

VIOLET – Nervous of offending. 30s.

AUSTIN – Overconfident, newly enlightened. 30s.

GEORGE O'DRISCOLL – Bullish. A pub philosopher. Late 30s.

ANNA O'DRISCOLL – End of her tether. A realist. 30s.

ELMORN JAMES – Proud, fourthright. 40s.

YOUNG CLARENCE JAMES – Shy and unsure. 13.

ESME – Middle Class, knows it. Late 20s.

ANGUS – Middle Class, doesn't know it. 30s.

TIME & SETTING

A Place for We is set in one building in Brixton, beginning in 1971 and spanning up until 2021.

AUTHOR'S NOTES

A slash [/] indicates overlap in speech.

A dash [–] indicates cut off speech.

An ellipsis […] indicates unvoiced thought.

For **CLARENCE** – Speech in **bold** indicates Trinidadian accent.

GLOSSARY

Big people – Older generation.

Buss-Up Shot – A Roti skin, resembling a bust up shirt. Also known as paratha.

Corbeau – A vulture/scavenger bird prevalent in Trinidad. An insult.

Crystals – Odour and fluid absorbing powder.

Dhalpouri – A Roti skin, stuffed with split peas.

Doubles – A Trinidadian street food consisting of Bara, Curry Channa and chutneys.

Jumbie – A spirit of a dead person, typically evil/vindictive.

Steups – Kissing of teeth.

ACT ONE

(A funeral directors. Nine Nights.)

(Downstage sits some comfortable chairs, an elegant table – a greeting area for the grieving to wait. To the left is the front door – a bell chimes whenever this door is opened.)

(Upstage is a large wooden desk. On its surface, a phone, a stack of cards and a computer. Upstage right is a door to the office.)

(Upstage left, a door to a small morgue, where the newly prepared, or yet to be prepared cadavers are kept before service.)

(A picture of Elmorn James, the founder of Nine Nights, sits on the back wall.)

(A candle sits against a pillar.)

(A stack of mail sits inside the front door.)

Scene One

(**KERON JAMES**, *wearing house clothes, enters through the front door.*)

(*He goes to the front door and picks up the mail and flicks through the envelopes, before pausing on one for a while.*)

(*He opens it. It takes a while for him to read.*)

(*He huffs loudly and shakes his head before placing the letter back in the envelope. He puts the letters on the table.*)

(*He goes to leave before remembering something. He turns back, lighting the candle. He huffs once more and exits to the morgue.*)

(*The song "Pon Di Cocky" by Aidonia plays.*)

(**KERON** *re-enters, wearing an apron and plastic gloves, pulling a coffin behind him.*)

(*He goes into the office, returning with a picture, some jewellery, a cross, a Trinidadian flag and a bottle of rum. Returning to the coffin, he opens it recoils and loudly sounds his disgust, slamming the lid down.*)

(*He takes a deep breath and opens the lid again and recoils once more, clearly holding vomit in his mouth. He tries to arrange the body but it's too much for him. He exits to the office.*)

(**CLARENCE JAMES**, *impeccably dressed, enters through the front door.*)

CLARENCE. Keron? *(Shouting.)* **Keron!**

KERON. In the back /

CLARENCE. **Keron! Keron! Keron! Keron!**

> *(The music switches off,* **KERON** *appears in the doorway, holding a packet of crystals.)*

KERON. Yes dad?

CLARENCE. **What di ass is this song?**

KERON. What?

CLARENCE. **Sit down pon di cocky?**

KERON. You like it?

CLARENCE. This is a nice old woman!

KERON. The beat is wicked though –

CLARENCE. Have some respect boy!

KERON. Just a song Dad. It's weird if I'm here alone and it's quiet.

CLARENCE. ***Pon di cocky?*** **Lawd farder forgive yuh fuh such foolishness!**

> **(CLARENCE** *steups.)*

If you have to play something, play something she would appreciate. She like Calypso –

> **(KERON** *approaches the coffin again, gags.)*

Wap'en to'yuh?

KERON. She stinks man!

CLARENCE. Since when are your lungs weak?

KERON. They ain't, but she does –

CLARENCE. She's dead. What, you want her to smell like a flower bed?

KERON. Come if you don't believe me.

(**CLARENCE** *comes closer and is hit.*)

CLARENCE. It's... It's not that bad. A little...pungent...but not that... **Why she look like so?**

KERON. Best I could do by myself.

CLARENCE. That's the best you could do? She's a little old woman.

KERON. She's meaty man.

(**CLARENCE** *grunts.*)

(*He goes to one side of the coffin,* **KERON** *to the other side. They rearrange the body until* **CLARENCE** *is satisfied.* **KERON** *promptly sprinkles the crystals in the coffin.*)

CLARENCE. Lid.

(**KERON** *quickly places the lid over the coffin.*)

KERON. Much better. I'll take her to the yard until we're ready for the service, let me get the car ready.

(**KERON** *grabs the car keys and exits.*)

(**CLARENCE** *stands over the coffin and puts his hand on it. He lingers. He opens it and places the lid down.*)

CLARENCE. **Rest in Power Miss Angie. Say hello to Daddy. I hope he... Sleep well.**

(**CLARENCE** *places the lid over the coffin and bows. He lingers next to it, as if he has more to discuss.*)

(**KERON** *comes through the door.*)

KERON. What you doing?

CLARENCE. **Nuttin...** Nothing.

KERON. Can I take her or would you like a further moment
alone?

> (**CLARENCE** *moves away.*)

> (**KERON** *wheels the coffin out the door.*)

> (**CLARENCE** *sits at the desk and begins to sift
> through the mail. He comes to the open letter.
> He takes it out and reads it.*)

CLARENCE. *(To himself.)* **Fucking Corbeau.**

> (**KERON** *comes through the door.* **CLARENCE**
> *stuffs the letter into his pocket.*)

KERON. She was more than a bit meaty. Dropped the car
down a couple inches... What you doing?

CLARENCE. What?

KERON. That...the letter you –

CLARENCE. **Private business, yuh understand? A man cyaa take
care of he private business in he own shop?**

> (**KERON** *backs off.*)

You hungry?

> (**KERON** *nods noncommittally.*)

Go to the doubles man for me. Two doubles, plenty
pepper.

KERON. You can't go?

CLARENCE. You really going to make a tired old West
Indian Negro walk through the winter conditions?

KERON. You were born in Battersea.

CLARENCE. **Is my *blood* from Battersea?** Go to the shop for
me.

KERON. Fine.

> (**KERON** *turns to go.*)

CLARENCE. And get me a couple of roti skin too. Couple Dhalpouri. Couple buss-up-shot.

KERON. Fine.

> (**KERON** *turns and leaves out of the door.*)

> (**CLARENCE** *takes the letter back out of his pocket.*)

CLARENCE. Yuh see this daddy? These people rel crazy. Offer anything to try and take we out –

> (**TASHA** *walks through the front door, carrying a binder.* **CLARENCE** *stuffs the letter back into his pocket, startled.*)

Oh gosh! Where you come from?!

TASHA. Morning to you too Dad. I *do* live here.. And work here.

CLARENCE. If you work here then why are you late?

TASHA. Had some stuff to get done for Keron didn't I. Where is he?

CLARENCE. Doubles man.

TASHA. Right, well, when he gets back, here's the pricing changes he asked for.

CLARENCE. What?

TASHA. He didn't tell ya?

CLARENCE. Nobody tell me a dyam thing about nuttin.

TASHA. Well here, I think they're good – just a couple of the wordings for stuff and that – are you sure he didn't tell ya?

(CLARENCE grunts.)

(TASHA hands over the binder. CLARENCE looks them over. He lowers the binder, confused.)

CLARENCE. What. Is. This?

TASHA. Pricing changes.

CLARENCE. Is this a joke?

TASHA. I don't think so. But you know him, his sense of humour is weird. He laughs at a lot of stuff and just, like, what's he laughing at, that's literally the opposite of –

CLARENCE. **This foolish boy!**

TASHA. So, I'm guessing you don't like it?

(CLARENCE steups.)

I think updates are good. Unless it's an iPhone, then you may as well just get a new phone.

CLARENCE. Update? Nine Nights is a traditional funeral directors, not a –

(KERON walks through the door.)

KERON. You ain't gonna be happy with – oh, hi babe. Didn't hear you leave this morning.

TASHA. All my ninja training babe.

(They kiss.)

Good luck.

KERON. With what?

CLARENCE. Damn right I'm not happy /

TASHA. He ain't happy.

KERON. I did the best I could.

> (**KERON** *hands him a roll in silver foil.*
> **CLARENCE** *looks from the roll to* **KERON**.)

Breakfast burrito.

CLARENCE. What is a breakfast borringo?

KERON. Burrito –

CLARENCE. Ah, they're well nice. That's from the new place down in the –

KERON. Yeah down in the village. Took over from Motaz.

TASHA. The butcher?

KERON. Yeah.

TASHA. At least that's one less person to stare at my chesticles. When did he go?

KERON. Couple months ago. He's gone down Sydenham, cheaper, more people to –

CLARENCE. What di ass is a breakfast borringo!

KERON. It's kind of like a Mexican roti.

CLARENCE. Eh-eh. I never ask for this!

KERON. Best I could do –

CLARENCE. Best I could do – what does that mean, best I could do?

KERON. Best I could… Island Life is closed, so that was the best I –

CLARENCE. What?!

KERON. It's closed. So a burrito was the best I –

CLARENCE. Closed? Since when?

TASHA. Recently. Couple weeks maybe.

CLARENCE. What?

TASHA. Yeah. That mental homeless man keeps trying to squat in there.

KERON. Jossiah ain't mental.

TASHA. The other day he was eating a pigeon in the square. With the feathers.

KERON. Yeah... Well... Innovation init. Waste not want not, all that kind of thing.

CLARENCE. Island Life really closed down? It's been here since nineteen sixty-eight. That long and it just close?

KERON. Like I said. Best I could do.

CLARENCE. And you got this from?

TASHA. From where Motaz was. New shop.

CLARENCE. Mexican? There's no Mexican people round here.

TASHA. People like Mexican food. It's fashionable.

(**CLARENCE** *throws the burrito in the bin.*)

KERON. What you do that for? That was eight pound!

CLARENCE. Eight pound! For bread and meat?

TASHA. And rice and peppers and Gua... Sorry.

CLARENCE. Ah doh wan this. Ah won't eat any of they food. Yuh understand?

KERON. *(Shrugging.)* Go hungry then.

(**KERON** *takes the burrito out of the bin and puts it back in the bag.*)

(**TASHA** *and* **CLARENCE** *look at him, disgusted.*)

What, we can afford to be throwing away money now?

(Beat.)

TASHA. To be fair, they are quite nice. Maybe you should –

CLARENCE. I don't want none of their food.

> (**CLARENCE** *steups and sulks off to the office.*)

KERON. Just leave him. He'll eat if he's hungry. Looks like we've got a fun day ahead.

TASHA. You know how people can get when their favourite places.

> (**KERON** *offers a burrito.*)

No thanks, I don't eat out of bins.

KERON. Babe, you're eating for two now remember?

> (**TASHA** *punches him in the arm.*)

TASHA. Alright dickhead, you want him to hear?

KERON. Gonna have to tell him sometime.

TASHA. Yeah but, babe, you have to pick your moments. That's your problem, you can't pick your moments.

KERON. Fine, well... Whenever you're ready.

TASHA. Bad luck to say too soon anyway.

KERON. Well, if we leave it too long –

TASHA. We ain't gonna leave it too long. Idiot. You think I'm just gonna rock up big belly and waddles and be like "guess who's gonna be a grandad?"

> (**KERON** *laughs, kisses her on the forehead and hands her the burrito. She switches hers with his.*)
>
> (*They start to eat.*)

You do realise this baby is going to be mostly white?

KERON. I'm aware of the science yes.

TASHA. But like, there's a chance it's gonna come out looking proper white. Like premium package white. Blue eyes, blonde hair.

KERON. Like a Nazi?

TASHA. Did you just call our baby a Nazi?

KERON. You're the one who said they might look like –

TASHA. Can you stop calling the baby a Nazi please. She's impressionable.

KERON. She?

TASHA. Feels like a she. Has a feminine energy.

KERON. What if it's just a very camp boy? I feel like you shouldn't be assuming their gender –

TASHA. It's a she!

(KERON *laughs.*)

Anyway, you'll probably want to prepare him for that.

KERON. It'll be fine. He don't care about stuff like that. Just be happy that his "legacy" is continuing.

(TASHA *grunts, then.*)

TASHA. Mum was saying that we're welcome to move in there. Much more space.

KERON. What's wrong with here?

TASHA. You want to raise a baby above an undertakers?

KERON. Why not?

TASHA. I'm sorry, shall we just give them a gun and send them into a school too? They'll be weird.

KERON. What about me?

TASHA. *You're* weird.

KERON. Yeah, well... Cross that bridge when we come to it.

(Pause.)

TASHA. Oh, pricing changes.

(She slides them over to him.)

I had a little look through them and I reckon they look alright. I thought you told your dad?

KERON. I *mentioned* it.

TASHA. Well, when I showed them to him –

KERON. He saw them?

TASHA. Weren't too happy –

KERON. What did he say?

TASHA. Well –

KERON. Oh, you know what? Forget what he... They look good.

TASHA. Yeah.

KERON. Updates it nicely, right?

TASHA. Wholeheartedly concur babe... Word of the day toilet paper.

KERON. So, what did he say?

TASHA. Didn't like it.

*(***CLARENCE*** bursts out of the office.)*

CLARENCE. What kind of Trinidadian go out for doubles and roti, and come back with one Mexican ting and try say /

KERON. It was the best I could do pops /

CLARENCE. Come back with nuttin and try say the shop gone.

KERON. OK, next time, I'll bring back nothing instead.

CLARENCE. What kind of Trinidadian bring back –

KERON. Please don't start –

CLARENCE. Shamed! This bwoi try an bring shame pon mi!

KERON. Stop being so dramatic please.

CLARENCE. Dramatic? Yuh tink ah dramatic?

KERON. Just a touch. Little, tiny morsel of...

> (**CLARENCE** *doesn't see the funny side.*)

Sorry.

CLARENCE. I don't want a sorry.

> (*Beat.*)

KERON. Tash, er... Tash said you saw the pricing changes?

> (**CLARENCE** *snorts.*)

So... That means you don't like it?

> (**CLARENCE** *steups.*)

What's wrong with a little update?

CLARENCE. Why you trying to fix something that isn't broke? Your leg works fine, you don't see me cutting it open and trying to fix it!

KERON. OK, fine... But say right, say, use my leg, my leg is perfectly fine, but what if you could add on some stuff to make it a little, like, if you can add on some wheels and a jet-pack and a storage unit, that would, that would make it a little bit better.

CLARENCE. What is this child talking about?

> (**TASHA** *shrugs, clearly used to this kind of thing.*)

KERON. I just mean... I only added – changed, changed a couple things to make it a little... Don't you think it's a little more you know.

TASHA. Up-to-date –

KERON. Up-to-date, exactly! Thank you babe /

TASHA. Welcome babe.

CLARENCE. It need updating fuh what?

KERON. Speak normally please.

CLARENCE. And now this bwoi talking about the way ah speaking. Bwoi, you schupid?

KERON. That's helpful.

CLARENCE. What, you want me to talk like Truck Lenny? That makes more sense to you? Awright then geezer, let's have it right, why you go and update something that didn't need updatin? Ya puddin.

TASHA. To be fair, that is an excellent impression.

KERON. I just thought that it could... You know. It hasn't been great these last few months... I thought this might attract some new clients or –

      (**CLARENCE** *snatches the folder out of his* **KERON***'s hand.*)

CLARENCE. Standard, special, super, ultimate, deluxe.

KERON. What's wrong with that?

CLARENCE. This is a traditional West Indian funeral directors, and you're making us sound like a damn car wash.

      (**TASHA** *stifles a laugh.*)

TASHA. Hadn't noticed that.

KERON. How?

CLARENCE. "Hello, welcome to Nine Nights. Oh, your mother has died, what a shame, could I interest you in our deluxe package?!"

TASHA. Well good at impressions Dad. Can you do Morgan Freeman?

CLARENCE. We want to show that we have experience with sending people off right, not ensuring they come away with a fresh wax!

(Beat.)

TASHA. OK well... I think I might go lie down... Yeah.

(TASHA *leaves.)*

(Beat.)

KERON. You know, you have a tendency to go a little overboard.

CLARENCE. Never say overboard to a West Indian!

KERON. I don't think it makes us look like a car wash at all.

CLARENCE. People see *that*, and they tink we rel stupid –

KERON. Can you let me talk please?

CLARENCE. Oh, ah forget ah talking to di marketing oracle. Forgive me, ah just a schupid old West Indian Negro, ah doh know nuttin about how this world works.

KERON. Please stop referring to yourself as Negro, I don't think that's acceptable anymore. Anyway... I think it updates us. We're a little stale –

CLARENCE. We're not bread. Stale! You stupid –

KERON. Let me talk!

(Beat.)

CLARENCE. OK. Talk nuh.

(Beat.)

KERON. Thank you. I just... I don't think that this makes us look bad. I think that this makes us look a little more, you know, current.

CLARENCE. Why we –

KERON. You said you would let me talk, so let me talk.

(**CLARENCE** *relents.*)

You know, it's a changing, like, you know with climate change and that and how they say the world is getting hotter and stuff. It's kinda like that. The climate, our climate here, is changing, and we kind of need to, you know, like if you don't adapt, then you die init, so, basically, I think that, like, we need to adapt to stay, like...proper, not proper but...current.

(Beat.)

CLARENCE. Nine Nights is a traditional West Indian funeral directors. We don't need to change nothing. People will always respect their tradition.

KERON. But how long until –

CLARENCE. You di owner?

KERON. No.

CLARENCE. Right!

KERON. So I don't get a say? I think –

CLARENCE. I don't care what you think! This is *my* business. I inherit it from my father. And I keep it going! Nine Nights is established, everybody knows about we. Why should we change?

KERON. *(Mumbling.)* Because everybody else is.

CLARENCE. Wah yuh say?

(Beat.)

KERON. Nothing... Nothing.

CLARENCE. Good. You are a Trinidadian. You must take care of we. Yes?

(Beat.)

KERON. Fine. I... I better finish preparing Miss Angie.

*(**CLARENCE** grunts.)*

*(**KERON** huffs and exits through the front door.)*

*(**CLARENCE** watches him go.)*

CLARENCE. Yuh see this daddy? This boy and he schupidness. Special, Deluxe. Oh gosh! If only yuh could... Well, ah doh have to tell yuh about it... Yuh watch it all... Anyways. Ah better make sure him doh play no more of that schupid music around Miss Angie. Foolishness... Deluxe. Who di ass this boy tink he is?

*(**CLARENCE** exits.)*

Scene Two

(A few months later.)

(Nine Nights. Night.)

(There is a party happening in the back, a nine night.)

(A mixture of traditional calypso and newer soca music can be heard. The candle flickers.)

(KERON sits at the desk. He absentmindedly taps along to the beat before catching himself and stopping.)

(TASHA enters, visibly showing now, bringing the sound of the party with her, and then shutting it out with the closing door.)

TASHA. You alright babe?

KERON. Yeah. Fine.

TASHA. You don't wanna come and...?

KERON. Nah.

TASHA. What's wrong?

KERON. You know it's just... It's weird init.

TASHA. What's weird?

KERON. Just... You know... She was like... She was here and then she's just... It's weird.

TASHA. Babe, death is the most un-weird thing. Happens to everyone. Part of life.

> *(TASHA strokes her belly.)*

KERON. Can you not make a death joke and then stroke your belly.

TASHA. So why don't you go and celebrate then?

KERON. Don't know really.

TASHA. They're all having loads of fun.

KERON. I'd rather not.

TASHA. And it's nearly midnight, soon they'll be eating the food and stuff.

KERON. I know.

TASHA. Your dad took the food off my plate, told me my belly is getting out of control. Can't hide it much longer you know babe.

KERON. When the time is right, we'll tell him.

TASHA. Honestly, why don't ya just have a look in? Any excuse for a good party normally you lot.

(A beat, then.)

KERON. *Them* lot.

(Beat.)

That's how they mourn init. *This* is how *I* mourn.

(Beat.)

TASHA. Why is it happening in here anyway?

KERON. What?

TASHA. In the shop. I thought they was meant to do it in the house, thought that was the whole point.

KERON. Normally they do.

TASHA. How's the spirit supposed to pass through if they ain't in the right house? It'll just get lost won't it?

KERON. It don't work that way babe. It's symbolic –

TASHA. Obviously it's symbolic, I ain't expecting a proper like spirit thing, what do you lot call them? A duppy?

KERON. Jumbie /

TASHA. A jumbie thing to come walk around and have a
chat am I?

KERON. Oh, no wait, a *jumbie* is a *bad* spirit, the *person* is
a *good* spirit, so just a normal spirit – anyway, they had
to do it here.

TASHA. Why?

KERON. The assisted living facility didn't reckon a party
would go down too well with the other residents.

(**TASHA** *nods fair enough. A beat, then –.*)

TASHA. So if the spirit can't find the body, does that mean
it's gonna haunt like, the assisted living place? Because
you never see that. That's weird init. If there is spirits
and ghosts and that, how come they never haunt
like blocks of flats or anything – it's always a creepy
mansion or like a random well or something.

(**KERON** *snorts.*)

Where's her kids?

KERON. Never had any. She helped raise me when Mum...
Yeah. Never had any.

(*Pause.*)

(**TASHA** *strokes her belly.*)

TASHA. How would you wanna go? If you had a choice?

KERON. Please give the belly stroking, death stuff a rest –

TASHA. How would you go?

(*Beat.*)

KERON. Never really thought about it if I'm honest.

TASHA. Everyone thinks about it.

KERON. I don't.

TASHA. Liar. I got two ways me.

KERON. Two ways?

TASHA. First one, right, first one, is being eaten by some massive like, a bear or shark or like, a massive pelican or something.

KERON. Why?

TASHA. Because right, if you think about it, then it's got to hurt, right, it's got to at least hurt to make it worth it.

KERON. To make it worth it?

TASHA. Makes perfect sense.

KERON. Bollocks.

TASHA. The second way –

KERON. This is insane –

TASHA. The second way right, the second way would, like, like if there was a terrorist attack or something and I'm in a building and the building gets like, a bit blown up or /

KERON. A bit blown / up?

TASHA. A plane or something, yeah a bit blown up, it can happen if it's a big building. But say a bit of it gets blown up and I'm gonna go anyway, then, because it has to hurt and that to make it worthwhile, then I would, like, I would do something crazy like... Like –

KERON. Jump?

TASHA. No, you bellend, more like...surf a table out of a window! Be a legend wouldn't I?

KERON. I don't think you know what *legend* means.

TASHA. How would you go?

KERON. Honestly, I have never –

TASHA. You're lying.

KERON. I'm not.

TASHA. Yeah you are, I can always tell when you're lying, you fiddle with your bits when you're –

KERON. No I don't!

(**TASHA** *looks at him.*)

(**KERON** *looks down to realise where his hand is.*)

Coincidence.

(*The candle flickers out.* **KERON**, *mechanically replaces it and relights it before returning to his seat.*)

TASHA. Never understood that.

KERON. What's to understand?

TASHA. The point. Like, what is the point, actually.

(**KERON** *shrugs.*)

TASHA. What's that supposed to mean then? You have so many shrugs, I don't know which one that's supposed to be.

KERON. I don't know.

TASHA. How can you not know? You always replace it, without fail, you must know why.

KERON. ...Tradition I guess. Sometimes you don't need to know, you just... Follow.

(**TASHA** *shrugs.*)

(*Pause.*)

I dunno. Maybe... Like a hero or something?

TASHA. I *knew* you thought about it, everyone thinks about it.

KERON. Yeah, but I don't like to.

>   *(Pause.)*

TASHA. What do you reckon it's like?

KERON. Don't reckon there's anything to it. You're here one minute and then... You ain't.

TASHA. Really?

KERON. Why you think the Pope's so rich? Because he knows there ain't nothing, so he's stacking money, because otherwise, he would be poor init?

TASHA. Doesn't make any sense babe.

KERON. Makes perfect sense. If he knew there was like, *something* after, then he would live life as a poor man because he would know how rich he would be at the end.

TASHA. Maybe.

KERON. Definitely.

TASHA. Well you can think your thing babe. I'll think mine.

KERON. You actually think there's something?

TASHA. Course I do. Why wouldn't there be anything?

KERON. You're worse than the big people. What, so you think that a spirit actually waits around for eight nights, just knocking about, and then, on the final night decides "that's it, had enough of all this" and departs into the spirit world?

TASHA. Didn't say I believed *that*.

KERON. Right then.

TASHA. But that don't mean that I think nothing happens. I dunno, do I –

KERON. That's the point babe. No-one knows. But they go on like they do.

TASHA. Maybe some people do.

KERON. Babe, nobody –

> (**CLARENCE** *bursts through the door. The song "Trini To The Bone" by David Rudder is playing.*)

KERON. Yeah, he knows, look at him. He knows it all.

TASHA. K –

CLARENCE. Of course ah know! Di rum ah get meh! Ah know it all!

KERON. Sounds like you're having a good time.

CLARENCE. Good? This is we duty. All about Miss John.

TASHA. Aw, that's nice.

KERON. Yeah, lovely –

TASHA. K, stop it –

KERON. I didn't say anything.

CLARENCE. Miss John, oh God! I miss she!

KERON. Here we go. Melodrama.

> (**TASHA** *nudges him to stop.*)

CLARENCE. She was a good woman yuh know. Always helping we to get by! She was a good woman –

TASHA. A great woman /

CLARENCE. Yeah bai, a great woman! She is one of the last. Last of a dying breed!

> (**KERON** *sighs loudly.*)

When we people come, she one of the first! They call them the Windrush generation!

KERON. Pops –

CLARENCE. And when this dyam country try send them back –
she stand up to everyone, for everyone. Miss John! She fight
fuh we, fuh all of we to have a place!

KERON. Here we go –

CLARENCE. "Some people say God is a Trini!" Oh gosh, that
true bai, if God a Trini Miss John be OK!

KERON. It's nearly midnight.

CLARENCE. Ah know bai! Ah come to find yuh both, say some
words yuh know.

KERON. I don't know about –

CLARENCE. Yes, yes, yuh being the quiet man, just come say a
few words for her.

KERON. I'm good.

> *(Pause.)*

> *(**CLARENCE** stares at him, puzzled.)*

I've already said stuff.

CLARENCE. Yuh never say nuttin for we.

KERON. Well, me and Tash, haven't I Tash, I was saying
stuff.

TASHA. He was.

CLARENCE. But he never say nuttin with *we*. Yuh cyaa come
and share yuh mind?

> *(**KERON** sighs loudly.)*

TASHA. K.

> *(Beat.)*

KERON. I don't want to.

(*Pause.*)

(**CLARENCE** *stops swaying and focusses on him.*)

CLARENCE. Oh-ho.

KERON. No, not like that I just –

CLARENCE. Yuh too good fuh us?

(**KERON** *sighs, looks to* **TASH** *for help. She offers pursed lips. Pause.*)

Miss John is one of di last of a dying breed.

KERON. Exactly.

CLARENCE. What yuh mean by that?

KERON. ...Nothing.

(**CLARENCE** *stares at him a while, first still, then swaying.*)

(*He shakes his head goes to the door. As he opens it, the chorus from the song "Trini" by Benjai plays.*)

CLARENCE. Yuh hear dat? Iz a Trini, yuh hear him say dat?

KERON. I hear it.

CLARENCE. This is we culture. This is what we do. And yuh cyaa come speak a couple words for... Yuh make me feel so shamed.

(**CLARENCE** *walks out.*)

(**KERON** *huffs.*)

TASHA. Well done.

KERON. What?

TASHA. You didn't have to be harsh.

KERON. I didn't say anything!

TASHA. Yeah, but you know. It's important to him. To *all* of them. You should be in there.

KERON. Why? Why the fuck does everyone always think I need to be doing something that I don't want to do?

TASHA. It's your culture babe –

KERON. It's their culture!

(*Pause.*)

TASHA. She *was* important to you, wasn't she?

KERON. Kind of question is that? Was she important to me, *course* she was important to me!

TASHA. Then makes sense for you to go and –

KERON. Babe, if I don't wanna go in there, I don't wanna go in there. It doesn't even make any sense.

TASHA. Thought you said sometimes stuff doesn't need to make sense and you just do it anyway.

KERON. That's different.

TASHA. OK.

(**TASHA** *stands up and begins to walk to the door.*)

KERON. Where you going?

TASHA. It's nearly midnight.

KERON. So?

TASHA. It's tradition.

KERON. Yeah, but it ain't nothing to do with, you don't even get it.

TASHA. It's not for me though, is it?

KERON. Course it's for you, who else is it for?

TASHA. Her.

KERON. What do you mean?

TASHA. If she believed it, then it's important. Doesn't matter what I think, it's not for me. It's for her. And them. You should come.

(*Beat.*)

KERON. No.

TASHA. Why not? You're not explaining anything, you're just throwing a tantrum.

KERON. Why do I have to explain myself? If I don't want to do something, I don't want to do it. If you don't want to smash a glass in my face, no further explanation needed. I just don't want to, OK?

(**TASHA** *sighs.*)

TASHA. K, honestly, you're going to regret if you don't –

KERON. You want me to explain? Cool, OK, boom. That woman, when my mum died, she gave up her life to help my dad and raise me. That's what she done. And I don't wanna go in there because the last time I went in there for one of these is when my mum... I ain't going in there and saying goodbye to another person with this dead tradition that ain't gonna be around much longer, I can't... I don't want to... I don't need to go and show off my grief so that other people feel... I can mourn just fine right here.

(*A beat, then –.*)

TASHA. OK... I... You never told me that.

(**KERON** *shrugs.*)

(**TASHA** *waits a moment, then walks to the door and opens it.*)

Sometimes, you have to do things for other people even if you don't understand why. Or do understand and don't want to. Miss John would've wanted you there. Just... It's nearly midnight. Think about it.

*(**KERON** doesn't respond.)*

*(**TASHA** waits, and then walks through the door.)*

*("Trini" begins to swell as **KERON** sits. He stands, thinking about his next move. He makes as if he's going to follow **TASHA** but catchess sight of the flickering candle. He watches it a while, before huffing and leaving out of the front door.)*

Scene Three

(The remnants of "Trini" begin to fade.)

(KERON *walks through the front door, carrying two pots of frozen yoghurt.)*

(As he enters, he stops and picks up a stack of mail and rifles through it.)

(He stops at one letter, opens it and reads.)

(He sighs loudly and visibly tenses, before stuffing the letter back in the envelope and returning it to the pile.)

(Mechanically, he goes towards the candle to light it but stops, thinking. He slowly lowers his hand and moves away.)

(TASHA, *heavily pregnant now, waddles out of the office. She sits down and exhales loudly.)*

KERON. Sexy –

TASHA. Fuck off! So?

KERON. Passion Fruit or Pink Guava?

TASHA. Guava.

> **(KERON** *hands her one of the tubs.)*

> **(TASHA** *goes to eat it, hesitates.)*

I've never had a Guava you know.

KERON. Seriously?

TASHA. I don't even know if this tastes like... I could eat this, and taste it, and then say oh, that's Guava, but it might not even taste the same. Taste it.

KERON. Why?

TASHA. You've had Guava ain't ya?

KERON. Yeah.

TASHA. So then you can taste and you can tell me if it tastes like what Guava is meant to taste like.

KERON. But I could just say it does, even if it didn't and you wouldn't know.

TASHA. What kind of knobhead would do that?

>   (**KERON** *tastes it.*)

Guava?

>   (*She tastes it.*)

KERON. Not really.

TASHA. That definitely tastes like Guava.

KERON. You've never even had a Guava.

TASHA. Yeah, but I reckon if I had a Guava, it would definitely taste like that. Science babe.

>   (**KERON** *laughs.*)

Plus, baby likes it. She's probably all tropical, so she would know what a Guava tastes like.

KERON. Said before she might be all white?

TASHA. Nah, way she's bouncing about, she's definitely got a tinge to her I reckon.

KERON. *Anyway.* We had any –

TASHA. Nothing.

KERON. No calls at all?

>   (**TASHA** *shakes her head.*)

>   (**KERON** *sighs.*)

He back yet?

TASHA. Still at the protest. I could hear Truck in the background. "We don't want none of your fucking posh shit round 'ere, you wrinkled ball bags! Pull ya fucking fingers out ya bumholes and leave us alone ya spanners". Bloody hilarious him.

KERON. It ain't gonna do anything.

TASHA. Never know babe. Be like that movie won't it, them three hundred blokes who beat the whole army.

KERON. Except they died and the army won anyway because they had the man power and the money and –

TASHA. They gave it a good go though. Can't ask more than that really.

KERON. That's all you care about init, that people gave it a good go?

TASHA. Obviously. That's all life is, babe. Have a good crack at it, do what you can, work hard, have a long rest in paradise, or the ground, or wherever you think you end up. Not that hard.

KERON. S'pose... Babe, I need to show you something.

TASHA. What?

KERON. Nothing weird.

TASHA. Are you sure? Last time you said that, you pulled out –

KERON. Nothing like that babe.

TASHA. What is it?

> (**KERON** *goes to the pile of letters and pulls out the opened one.*)

> (*He takes out the letter and hands it to her.*)

(**TASHA** *reads through, sounds her amazement.*)

That's a lot of zeros.

KERON. He's fucking nuts if he doesn't –

TASHA. Way more than the last one.

KERON. Yeah, way more... Wait. What?

TASHA. Way more than the last one.

(*Pause.*)

KERON. You knew?

TASHA. There's been loads of 'em.

KERON. Loads?

TASHA. Here.

(**TASHA** *opens the drawer on the desk and pulls out a pile of letters.*)

(**KERON** *starts to look through them.*)

(*Pause.*)

(**KERON** *slams the drawer shut.*)

Don't be so loud, you'll wake the baby.

KERON. What are you talking about?

TASHA. Oh brilliant, she's kicking away now. What's the matter with you?

KERON. Him, just... He can't keep just... Just...

(**KERON** *stifles a roar.*)

TASHA. It'll be alright babe.

KERON. Yeah? What we gonna do when there's an extra mouth to feed? What we gonna do then?

TASHA. Probably should have had these fears before you forgot to pull out.

KERON. I'm serious, we've got no... We can't keep on like this.

TASHA. Business might pick up.

KERON. He's going to drag us under. I've tried to make him see sense, but he just... He's happy being blind to it.

TASHA. You've talked to him about it?

KERON. Sort of. Said how everyone is moving out and maybe we do the same.

TASHA. And?

KERON. "Schupid bai! Yuh fucker yuh, this is we place".

       (Beat.)

I've been thinking about it. I reckon, realistically now, *realistically*, we have, like, two options. Yeah two proper options. No, three, three proper ones.

TASHA. Enlighten me babe.

KERON. OK, number one, worst case, go from bad to good, worst case, is that he takes one of those offers, sells up and we move somewhere, get a new kinda business or something like, and then he can retire if he wanted to.

TASHA. He ain't old enough to retire though.

KERON. Yeah, but imagine, he can go into early retirement, go to Trinidad, buy up some land and build something, he would love that. That's worst case, and that's not even bad.

TASHA. What kinda new business though?

KERON. I been thinking, reckon I might have come up with a banger. You know how kids are little yeah?

(**TASHA** *grunts.*)

When you're teaching them to write, you give them regular sized pencils. Right?

(**TASHA** *nods.*)

So I'm thinking, because kids are little. Small pencils.

(**TASHA** *grunts again.* **KERON** *nods.*)

TASHA. That's your idea?

(**KERON** *grunts.*)

What's the other one.

KERON. That's a great idea!

TASHA. No it's not. It's stupid. Just sharpen the pencil smaller. What's the other option for him?

KERON. Fine, option number two, which I reckon is the most viable, is that we stop all this Caribbean vibe stuff and change it into a regular funeral directors.

TASHA. But then it wouldn't be Nine Nights anymore.

KERON. Exactly. It would make more sense right?

TASHA. Don't think your dad would go for that.

KERON. Course he wouldn't, but it's an option. This would make our client base a lot more...sustainable...it makes sense.

TASHA. Three?

KERON. We take Nine Nights, the franchise, and relocate it to somewhere...where it will...make sense.

TASHA. Babe... This is Brixton. Even when your cousins came over, said it was like little Jamaica.

KERON. How long ago was that? Brixton ain't *Brixton* no more.

TASHA. Where would we go then?

KERON. I dunno...

TASHA. What about like the Windrush generation and all that, they all came *here*.

KERON. And they've died here, we've fucking buried them all! And the ones we haven't got bloody sent back by the home office, didn't they. If they're all gone, how are we meant to –

(*A bell chimes as the front door opens.*)

(*An attractive, bohemian couple,* **AUSTIN** *and* **VIOLET,** *enter.*)

TASHA. Oh. Hello.

VIOLET. Hi. Erm, is this, this is a funeral directors, right?

KERON. Yes. Nine Nights.

AUSTIN. Never been in here. Not that I would, I mean, you know, not exactly a place that you hope to frequent.

KERON. I get what you mean.

AUSTIN. But no very, you know, very nice. Really nice place.

TASHA. Thanks. People don't always tend to notice places like this. They're quite... –

KERON. Understated /

TASHA. Understated, yeah.

KERON. How can we help?

VIOLET. Oh, right, erm...you're a funeral directors? I mean, of course you are but...you do funerals, obviously... And you're properly, I mean, you're well established?

TASHA. Been serving the community since nineteen seventy-one.

VIOLET. Wow, so, so, you've been here a while, you know what you're doing?

KERON. We do, yeah.

VIOLET. OK. Good. That's good, that sounds good doesn't it?

AUSTIN. Sounds good to me.

VIOLET. Yeah, good.

TASHA. Good.

VIOLET. Right then…

(*Pause.*)

TASHA. So…what's the…

(**TASHA** *gestures.*)

VIOLET. I'm sorry?

KERON. Situation.

VIOLET. I don't, what situation?

TASHA. The situation…the one that's brought you in here today.

AUSTIN. Who's died you mean?

TASHA. We can't really come out and say that. Disrespectful.

KERON. We say "the situation".

AUSTIN. Yes. Makes sense.

(*Pause.*)

KERON. So?

VIOLET. So?

TASHA. The situation?

VIOLET. Oh, right, sorry, I don't really, I mean, I haven't really go that much experience in, you know.

KERON. That's completely fine. Why don't you sit down.

TASHA. You can take your time, there's no rush.

VIOLET. Right.

(VIOLET *and* AUSTIN *sit down.*)

Right. My great auntie, or great great auntie, I'm not actually totally sure how great a relation she was.

KERON. Right.

AUSTIN. We'll just say auntie –

VIOLET. Yeah, let's say auntie, it's all the same anyway isn't it, family is family and all.

TASHA. Family *is* family.

VIOLET. So, anyway. My auntie died a few days ago.

KERON. I'm sorry to hear that.

AUSTIN. Oh, no, no, please, she had a good innings.

VIOLET. Ninety-six.

AUSTIN. More of a relief than anything –

VIOLET. Erm, excuse me, this is my family we're talking about here.

AUSTIN. Yes, but those were your, you said it was a relief, not me.

VIOLET. I know that, but it's my auntie, so it's...look it doesn't matter. Anyway, my auntie died a few, and we're looking for, I don't know, something suitable for her... Like an arrangement or...

AUSTIN. A nice little send off.

TASHA. We can do that.

AUSTIN. Excellent.

TASHA. Was there anything you had in mind in particular?

VIOLET. Oh...erm... I think...she was very into this new age vibe, sort of...

TASHA. I'm not sure I follow.

AUSTIN. We read that you can get those renewable coffins now. Like, a wicker one that you get cremated in. Or one of those pods? Where they plant you and use your remains to grow a tree or something like that. Do you...

TASHA. That's not really our forte.

(**KERON** *mouths "Forte?"*)

AUSTIN. Right.

VIOLET. I think, yeah, I think she'd love the pod. She loved gardening.

TASHA. Right. We usually focus on a more...*traditional* service.

AUSTIN. Right. Sorry, I'm not sure what you're, are you saying that you can't provide –

KERON. Whatever you want, I'm sure we can make the arrangements.

TASHA. We can?

KERON. Yeah, course we can.

(*Pause.*)

TASHA. Right. OK. Good then.

AUSTIN. Excellent.

KERON. We'll be able to make something work, I'm sure.

VIOLET. I mean, possibly, maybe the traditional way would be more... I don't...what would traditional entail?

KERON. Well, we normally, but we don't have to of course, we normally practice the tradition of Nine Nights.

AUSTIN. Ah, so that's why it's called...

(**KERON** *nods and smiles.*)

And what is Nine Nights?

KERON. Kind of like a wake. People come together to celebrate the person that's died.

AUSTIN. Over nine nights? Clever.

KERON. That's how long the spirit takes to settle before it can depart to the next world.

AUSTIN. Fascinating. And that's African?

TASHA. Caribbean.

VIOLET. I don't think, I mean, Auntie Elsie, she was quite...

AUSTIN. Simple.

VIOLET. Not in a bad way.

AUSTIN. She just didn't like a fuss over anything.

VIOLET. Yes, I mean...sorry I've...never done this before. It's all a bit...

KERON. That's fine. Take your time.

VIOLET. I think that, anything too, you know, traditional, I don't think that she would've wanted that.

KERON. We can do whatever suits you.

VIOLET. Great. Thank you.

(*Beat.*)

AUSTIN. So, do we need to, is there anything we need to give you?

KERON. A couple of details, and we can give you some time alone while you talk things over. You can take all the time you need.

AUSTIN. I don't think we'll need too much time.

VIOLET. No...but you know, best to probably, just to, you know, sit down and talk things through.

AUSTIN. Of course.

KERON. Why don't you go and sit in the office? Take all the time you need.

> *(**KERON** leads **VIOLET** and **AUSTIN** through to the office.)*
>
> *(**TASHA** sits at the desk.)*
>
> *(**KERON** returns.)*

TASHA. What the actual fuck?!

KERON. *That* was called providing for the clientele. That's what Nine Nights should do. And by the way, Forte? Who are you, Stephen Fry now?

TASHA. Word of the day toilet paper – don't change the subject. Where we gonna get a pod thing from? Don't even know what they're called.

KERON. They're called eco-pods. All the rage right now.

> *(**TASHA** shakes her head.)*

There's no point in maintaining this dead tradition!

TASHA. What's your dad going to say?

KERON. I don't care. Once I sort everything without him, he'll see that this is exactly –

> *(**CLARENCE** comes through the door.)*
>
> *(**KERON** and **TASHA** freeze.)*
>
> *(Pause.)*
>
> *(**CLARENCE** struts around triumphantly.)*

CLARENCE. Yuh cyaa ask how it go?

TASHA. How did it –

CLARENCE. We chase them off!

TASHA. What...what happened?

CLARENCE. You should have seen us. Me and Truck, Truck is crazy you know! They came with their clipboards and their hard hats and shiny shirt. And everyone was just out and ready to stop them. Me and Truck was at the front. They come, and they stand up in we face and ask us "are we going to have a situation?" I never say nothing, I just stand and stare.

But Truck, he's never the person to just stay silent like so, so he reaches into his pocket, he pull out a can of Lynx. **Ah tinking what di ass this man doing?** Fucking hell Truck, not the time to making sure you smell criss. But then, **oh god! This man rel crazy!** Then, he pulls out a lighter, and I'm thinking, what is this crazy man doing.

TASHA. Oh, he didn't –

CLARENCE. He start spraying the Lynx right at the shiny man and he put the lighter in front and click it and the ting start burning!

TASHA. He's a bloody headcase that one.

CLARENCE. **Ah telling yuh!** And he start waving the thing around, he start up another one, so he has two Lynx flamethrowers flying at the shiny man, and they back away. And Truck, he just look at the man cool and say "This is our faaking ouse! You faaking try and take it, ya pudding!" **And the man them back away rel scared.**

TASHA. And then what happened?

CLARENCE. Truck run after them shouting. Chase them all the way to Stockwell.

> (**CLARENCE** *laughs.*)

KERON. Well done then.

CLARENCE. You see, we have to fight for we right to live! You should have seen me boy! Chasing after them people. Just like when the Carib chase off the people when they first come.

KERON. I'm sure.

CLARENCE. We come from a fighting people, you know. The Carib was a fighting people. It was their tradition. We have to fight to keep we place, we have to respect we tradition, you know –

> (KERON *makes a shush sign with his hand.*)

Are you shushing, is he shushing me?

KERON. We've got some clients inside.

CLARENCE. Oh, you should have tell me. Who is it? Mr Fleming? Last time I see him he was looking frail.

KERON. Nah, not Mr Fleming –

CLARENCE. Don't tell me Miss Williams? She barely get to use her new hip.

KERON. It's...you don't know them.

> (*Pause.*)

> (CLARENCE *smiles.*)

What?

CLARENCE. You see. I know. I *always* know. People will always respect tradition. No matter –

> (CLARENCE *notices the candle he stares at it.* KERON *doesn't move.*)

TASHA. Right, shall I just –

> (CLARENCE *motions for silence. He walks over slowly, looking at the candle, touching the dry wax.*)

CLARENCE. You never light it this morning?

> (**KERON** *doesn't respond.*)

Boy, you hear me? I ask you a question –

> (**VIOLET** *and* **AUSTIN** *come out of the office.* **CLARENCE** *quickly goes into proprietor mode.*)

VIOLET. All done now I... Oh. Hello.

CLARENCE. Hello Miss...?

VIOLET. Wilcox. Violet.

CLARENCE. Miss Wilcox. Let me introduce myself, my name is Clarence, the owner of Nine Nights. I'm very sorry to learn of your loss, but let me assure you, you are in very good hands and we will do everything to make this as simple and easy as possible.

VIOLET. Thank you.

AUSTIN. Brilliant.

VIOLET. We were...your colleagues were taking care of us really well, we feel very –

AUSTIN. Comfortable.

CLARENCE. Good.

KERON. I can...you can go and sort yourself out after the protest and –

CLARENCE. No, no, I always make sure that we are looked after properly.

> (**CLARENCE** *smiles at* **AUSTIN** *and* **VIOLET.**)

AUSTIN. You were at the protest?

CLARENCE. Indeed I was, yeah. **Have to show them you know.**

VIOLET. I didn't even know there was a protest.

CLARENCE. Not massive, but a nice size.

VIOLET. What was it about?

KERON. I don't think, I mean, maybe that's a conversation for another time –

AUSTIN. Please, we like to help serve the community as much as the next man. Or woman. Person.

CLARENCE. These people they come over, they buy up one bit in the village, and then, get this...they want to build a *coffee-cocktail boudoir*.

(*Beat.*)

AUSTIN. Right. And, just so I'm, you are against that?

CLARENCE. Of course! Who wants that kind of foolishness round here?

VIOLET. I'd quite... I mean, that sounds like it would add something to the community. Something different and...

AUSTIN. Fresh –

VIOLET. Fresh. Yes, exactly.

(*Beat.*)

CLARENCE. Fresh?

VIOLET. Well, yeah, you know...nice bit of culture and, something new. Yeah, would be nice.

CLARENCE. How you mean?

AUSTIN. Well, something like, it could only be good for the surroundings. Generate a big income, create employment opportunities –

CLARENCE. What about taking business away from the people already here?

AUSTIN. How would it do that?

CLARENCE. That place come here, who is going to go to
    Sonny's? His bar been here since nineteen sixty-five.
    Who going to Miss Phillip's cafe?

KERON. Maybe we should get all this sorted out and then
    continue with...yeah?

>   *(Beat.)*

CLARENCE. Yeah, yeah, sorry, sorry I just, get all passionate
    and emotional you know?

AUSTIN. Not a problem.

VIOLET. No, standing up for your beliefs, it's commendable.

>   *(Beat.)*

KERON. I can take it from here.

CLARENCE. I will stay and help.

>   *(Pause.)*

KERON. OK, erm...shall we sit down.

>   *(They all sit, but for **CLARENCE**.)*

>   *(**KERON** looks over the form.)*

OK... Right... Right... Well this all looks very...yep, very
doable.

VIOLET. You know, something, just, something nice and –

AUSTIN. Simple /

VIOLET. Simple, exactly.

KERON. Yep.

VIOLET. I think the eco-element, she'd like that.

>   *(**KERON** nods.)*

CLARENCE. You like the name of the services?

AUSTIN. I'm sorry?

KERON. Dad –

CLARENCE. I'm just asking if they like what the services are entitled. You like them?

KERON. Dad, please –

CLARENCE. I'm only asking a question.

KERON. We've developed, they've got a personalised package. I can handle it Dad, seriously.

(**CLARENCE** *backs off.*)

KERON. Right, so erm, is there anything specific you might want?

AUSTIN. Such as?

KERON. Music, any special readings –

VIOLET. Maybe some people can speak. And a poem?

AUSTIN. She'd like a poem.

(**KERON** *nods.*)

VIOLET. Right. Great. So is, I mean, is there anything else that we need to...

KERON. Let us start making the arrangements and then we can call with anything else that –

CLARENCE. What part of the Caribbean your people come from?

VIOLET. Pardon?

KERON. Dad –

CLARENCE. I only ask a question –

KERON. I know that, but I'm handling it, just let me –

AUSTIN. Actually, we're, her family, they're from Dorset.

(Pause.)

KERON. Yeah, we actually had that conversation before you came in Dad –

CLARENCE. So how you know about Nine Nights?

KERON. Dad, seriously –

CLARENCE. Boy, hush your mouth and let the people answer the question.

VIOLET. Well we...we saw the sign and we were in need of assistance and...we thought, you know, a community place might be...

> *(**CLARENCE** smiles.)*

CLARENCE. You see that, boy! Community always come together for the greater good!

> *(**CLARENCE** shakes **VIOLET** and **AUSTIN**'s hand.)*

AUSTIN. Yes, well, community, it's important, you know?

CLARENCE. Yes sir, most important ting. Community support!

> *(**AUSTIN** nods his head, laughs. **CLARENCE** quickly moves over and relights the candle.)*

*(To **KERON**.)* See that? I telling you. Tradition always maintain. They coming in here, learning about we culture, following the nine night tradition –

KERON. Can we do this later? Please?

CLARENCE. It's a good thing.

> *(**CLARENCE** turns to **AUSTIN** and **VIOLET**.)*

You know, my son, he think that our tradition is outdated and... But when you do it, you will see what it mean. You will feel how the spirit take you.

(Beat.)

VIOLET. Right. That's... I'm sorry, I don't understand.

CLARENCE. He never explain?

AUSTIN. I thought, we discussed the service, and that we didn't want to –

TASHA. They're going to have a small, simple service.

CLARENCE. More intimate.

KERON. No, just...a little thing. No big rituals or...small and simple.

CLARENCE. No nine nights?

KERON. ...

(Pause.)

*(***CLARENCE*** stares at ***KERON***, stung to the core.)*

AUSTIN. Is that, I mean, we were told that would be fine.

CLARENCE. We... I don't...

AUSTIN. Is everything, I mean, if there's anything else we need to talk about...

CLARENCE. I'm sorry but... We won't be able to offer you our services for this ceremony...ah can recommend somebody that would be able to help in this regard.

VIOLET. Is there, I don't understand, is there a problem –

CLARENCE. No problem. It's just, that's not what we do here.

KERON. Dad, I'm handling it –

CLARENCE. This is a traditional West Indian funeral directors. So the services that we carry out are traditionally West Indian.

VIOLET. Right. I still don't...

CLARENCE. Ah sorry but, ah don't think we will be able to provide the services that you need. I can refer you to another director who would be more...flexible.

KERON. Dad –

AUSTIN. That's discrimination.

CLARENCE. Ah doh find so.

AUSTIN. You're saying we can't use your services unless we're of West Indian –

CLARENCE. Yuh doh have to be. Yuh have to respect the tradition. Same if yuh go to a Catholic undertaker asking for a humanist service. Ah afraid we cyaa do that.

AUSTIN. This is ridiculous.

KERON. No, look, listen I'm sure we can sort something –

CLARENCE. Ah sorry you feel that way.

AUSTIN. If you think that we're just going to, I am going to write to the office of trading standards –

VIOLET. Austin, Austin, stop. Just...

(*Pause.*)

If you could recommend... I mean, we just want something...

CLARENCE. Ah understand. That's not what we do here. Plenty people do, but not us.

(**CLARENCE** *writes down a name and number on a piece of paper and hands it to* **VIOLET.**)

Very sorry for your loss. Ah hope yuh auntie find the peace that she deserve.

VIOLET. Thank you.

(**VIOLET** *and* **AUSTIN** *exit, arguing on the way out.*)

(Pause.)

TASHA. Reckon I should probably leave you two...things to chat about eh?

(Neither **CLARENCE** *or* **KERON** *respond.)*

OK...babe I'll... I'll be...go and find something to do and...might go and see Truck and his flamethrowers or...yeah.

*(***TASHA*** *exits.)*

(A long pause.)

CLARENCE. You happy?

KERON. Not at all.

(Pause.)

CLARENCE. Yuh little fucker yuh.

KERON. Dad, I had that!

CLARENCE. What did you have?

KERON. *Them!* I had them, they were going to use us, and you come in and –

CLARENCE. No, they didn't want to use we. They wanted something soulless.

KERON. But I had them.

CLARENCE. You're a fool if you think you –

KERON. We haven't had a fucking client for what? A month? Six weeks?

CLARENCE. Business a little slow, but it always pick up around winter.

KERON. That's not why the business is fucking slow!

CLARENCE. It's warmer, people hang on a little, and then when the cold come –

KERON. Which people?! Tell me which ones?

CLARENCE. The same people Nine Nights was built to
serve.

KERON. But they're gone! They're all fucking –

CLARENCE. **Watch your mouth you know.**

> (*Pause.*)

KERON. They're all gone, Dad.

CLARENCE. No... No, they're not, they're...there's still Miss
Angie. Mister Fleming is...and then there's Rock and
Jamesy and –

KERON. Rock lives in Newcastle now. Jamesy moved back
to Trinidad. We buried Miss Angie months ago. Don't
you get it?

CLARENCE. We will be fine.

KERON. All them people, the ones that brought the
tradition over –

CLARENCE. And there's the next generation of people, the
people like me, we always respect we –

KERON. So what, we have to wait years for your lot to die
to be able to afford a fucking loaf of bread?

CLARENCE. **Ay bai! Ah tell yuh, watch yuh mout!**

KERON. You know it's true! You know you do, but you just
don't want to admit it.

CLARENCE. So what? What you think we should do then?

KERON. We should be doing what you wouldn't let me do
just now.

> (**CLARENCE** *shakes his head.*)

Why not?

CLARENCE. Because that is not Nine Nights.

KERON. Why can't we do both?

CLARENCE. No.

KERON. Then we should leave. Either sell up or –

CLARENCE. Ah tell yuh no!

> *(Pause.)*

> **When my father first come here, he have nothing. Nothing except the community of other people like him. There was unity.**

> **That is what Nine Nights stand for. All different people had become one. You understand?**

KERON. But these ain't the same people.

CLARENCE. Boy, you don't even know what you're speaking.

KERON. Thing with tradition is that it either changes or gets forgotten, right? Those people with the tradition that you respect so much are either dead or gone. You see any West Indians? Where are they? Are they hiding in all the rum shacks along Electric Avenue? Are they in the dances? There ain't no rum shacks and there ain't no dances. There ain't none of you here any more. It's been made pretty clear that you don't belong. From people leaving to being forced out by the government. There's none of you left. I mean, fucking hell, you got other people trying to buy places up and the only way you can chase them off is with a homemade flamethrower!

> *(Beat.)*

CLARENCE. How you mean *you*?

KERON. What?

CLARENCE. You say to me there ain't none of *you* here anymore.

KERON. West Indian.

CLARENCE. And you are what?

KERON. I ain't West Indian.

CLARENCE. Look at you. You cyaa see it? You're a Trini.

KERON. I am of Trinidadian heritage, but I'm not a Trini.

CLARENCE. Yuh confused –

KERON. I'm not confused! When I go there, what do they call me? English Muffin, not Trini boy, not red skin, *English Muffin*. That make me a Trini?

CLARENCE. Yuh think you're English?

KERON. I never said that.

CLARENCE. So, yuh not Trini, yuh not English, what yuh are?

KERON. I'm a Londoner. Not English, not Trini. Both and neither at the same time.

CLARENCE. Yuh confused –

KERON. *You're* confused! You weren't even born there, and you think yourself a Trini.

(*Beat.*)

CLARENCE. Iz ah Trini to de bone. To de bone bai, yuh understand? The blood flowing through meh vein, meh heart. From meh head top to meh foot bottom. Trini. What is this? Ah do somethin t'yuh? Yuh deny yuh people, we culture. Yuh modda would be shame of yuh.

KERON. What are you talking about, she was English. You met her down Tooting!

CLARENCE. But she knew *you* were a Trini.

KERON. She only did all of that to keep you and Elmorn happy!

CLARENCE. It was more than that. She *knew*. How yuh can even say yuh not Trini? No matter what, yuh won't be one of *them*.

KERON. And that works both fucking ways. I'll never belong here, I'll never belong there.

CLARENCE. Yuh hate yourself that much to say these things to me? Ah do someting to yuh?

KERON. Why do I have to hate myself to speak the truth?

CLARENCE. The truth? OK, let's talk truth. My grandchild, yuh do that to hurt me, yes?

KERON. What the hell are you talking about now?

CLARENCE. Ah walk down the street, people tinking "oh there's a black man stole a white baby". Yuh do that to make me feel shame and fear and all them tings, yes?

KERON. ...Are you... Oh my god. You're mental. You married a white woman yourself!

CLARENCE. It's not the same. Yuh know when you breed up Tash that when that child grow up, they will be opposite to me.

Yuh going to raise them as a little *English muffin*? Tell them some crazy stories about mad immigrant pops?

KERON. You don't know what you're saying, do you? *You were born here*, you can't be an immigrant –

CLARENCE. But ah hurt like they hurt! When they send we people back, ah hurt the same way! Their blood is my blood and if it came down to it, ah would be with them rather than here! Ah may be born here, but ah am not from here and ah will *never* belong outside of *my* community. All ah can do is uphold the traditions that shape me and my people. What shape *we* community.

KERON. But there is no community anymore, the community is the people and the people are leaving –

CLARENCE. This is where we belong! This is we home –

KERON. We don't belong here anymore! The climate is fucking changing. There ain't no West Indian restaurants opening, but there's champagne bars and coffee cocktail...what does that tell you? People were dragged out kicking and screaming from this country, and everyone turned a blind eye when you think about it. Why? Because everybody is thinking that your time is done. You need to open your eyes, stop letting your head get fool up in the fucking past! They ain't here no more, people don't want us here no more, people don't want any of this traditional fuckery any –

(**CLARENCE** *slaps* **KERON**.)

(*Pause.*)

CLARENCE. This is we life. This is everything there is for we. Without it, we die.

KERON. Yeah? Well with it, I can't live. What kind of life is this? Fuck pops, I've got a baby about to...what am I supposed to do with...maybe? Maybe someone dies so we can live? What am I supposed to do with that? I can't go on waiting for people to die so I can live.

(*Long pause.*)

CLARENCE. This is all I know.

KERON. It doesn't have to be. It's only that way if you let it be that way.

(*Beat.*)

CLARENCE. Without this place, what is my life?

(*Pause.*)

KERON. With it, what's mine?

(*Pause.*)

(**KERON** *walks out.*)

(**CLARENCE** *watches the door, then looks to the candle flickering, then turns to face the picture of Elmorn.*)

(He walks to the desk and pulls out the wad of letters.)

(He looks over some, and then starts to tear them apart.)

(Blackout.)

ACT TWO

(A traditional English pub. The Queen's Head. 1971.)

(Small round tables are dotted around. Some have half-drunk pints of beer on them. There's an ashtray on every table, some overflowing with cigarettes and mounds of ash.)

(The bar is bare, and apart from the tables and ashtrays, there is a feeling of emptiness. There are several open cardboard boxes dotted around.)

(The air is smokey, the last of the customers have just left the pub, yet their smoke lingers behind them, remnants of their presence hanging in the air.)

(Framed football kits, and several pictures of a child hang on the wall.)

(A candle burns on a pillar.)

Scene One

(The Temptations' "Just My Imagination"
plays on a radio.)

*(***GEORGE*** *cleans glasses and ashtrays off the*
tables. He's slow and lethargic, but deliberate
and mechanical. He stops, crossing his arms
and pondering.)

*(***ANNA*** *wipes down tables and the bar. She*
stops and stares at ***GEORGE***. *She huffs and*
switches off the radio.)

(A beat, then –.)

GEORGE. Do you reckon I could fight a cow?

*(***ANNA*** *stares at him, sighs.)*

What?

ANNA. This is all I bloody need now.

GEORGE. What do you mean?

ANNA. You. And your...*you-ness.*

GEORGE. You-ness? What does that mean, you-ness –

ANNA. Honestly, only on tonight of all nights would you
think a thought like that. Who asks a question like
that?

GEORGE. What's wrong with it?

ANNA. There's any manner of things wrong with it George.
For a start, you haven't said a word since we shut them
doors, which means you must have been thinking
about that for at least twenty minutes, which in itself
is loopy –

GEORGE. Far from loopy, / perfectly

ANNA. And on a night like tonight, you'd rather / think about...

GEORGE. Perfectly legitimate question.

ANNA. What even made you think of that?

GEORGE. It was just on my mind.

ANNA. Just on your mind?

GEORGE. Well, yeah. I think stuff.

ANNA. Well, you *should* be thinking about the task at hand, which is packing everything away before we have to –

GEORGE. I was talking to Tel, and he was telling me he's packing it all in at the market to open a dairy farm in Essex.

ANNA. A dairy farm?

GEORGE. And I thought that sounds alright. So I ask, how do you get in to that then? He goes Reggie knows a bloke down Billericay who's trading some cattle –

ANNA. Reggie knows someone in Billericay? He's not ever left South London, has he?

GEORGE. Sorry, not Reggie-Reggie, Reggie-Digits, him what don't have any thumbs – will you just let me tell ya? Anyway, Tel says that Reggie-Digits knows a bloke. So Tel starts asking questions, and he finds out that there's a lot of money in the dairy business, because people are always gonna be needing milk ain't they? Tea, cheese, butter – basics of life and that will never change. So he asks more questions and starts liking the idea – then he starts asking around. He finds out he's got a cousin out in Tiptree with a lot of land. Tel calls him up, asks if he wants to go in to business, cousin says OK.

Tel rings up Reggie-Digits' mate, says he wants a dozen cows to start up – some Holstein Friesan, a Guernsey, a Jersey, an Aberdeen Angus and a Longhorn, but who knows what he wants with that.

ANNA. Sorry, when did you become an expert in cows?

GEORGE. I happen to be a very knowledgeable individual, actually. He tells me all of that, and then I said he's gonna have his hands full because cows can be tricky customers, and he says he'd have no problem because he once knocked out Henry Cooper when they sparred together a few years back. And that is what led me to my own personal analysis of the situation, thus leading me to ask that question.

ANNA. Right. I see.

GEORGE. Do you reckon I could?

ANNA. Fight a cow?

GEORGE. You seen how good I am at handling the wronguns that turn up in here sometimes.

ANNA. A drunk teenager is very different to a half a tonne beast George. Now, will you stop prevaricating and help me clean up?

GEORGE. Prevaricating? Since when do you say –

ANNA. George!

> (**GEORGE** *throws up his hands and resumes his task of clearing glasses off tables.* **ANNA** *resumes wiping down the tables that have already been cleared.*)

GEORGE. *(Mumbling.)* I reckon I could.

> (**ANNA** *shoots him a stern look, which snaps him back to his task. He picks up a half-drunk pint glass and surveys it in the light.*)

Who does that, eh?

ANNA. Sorry?

GEORGE. Generally got an excellent understanding of human behaviours, wouldn't you say?

ANNA. Wouldn't say excellent –

GEORGE. I'm a good bloke. I understand everyone's got their little ticks and quirks. Got an excellent understanding of that.

ANNA. *Hardly* excellent –

GEORGE. But for the life of me, I cannot get my head around –

ANNA. What are you bleeding banging on about?

(**GEORGE** *walks over and puts the pint down in front of* **ANNA.**)

What am I looking at?

(**GEORGE** *motions to the pint glass.*)

And what's that then?

GEORGE. What do you think that is?

ANNA. Well, I know I might not be the sharpest knife in the drawer, certainly not a bovine expert or an excellent understander of people like yourself, but according to what I'm seeing, and please, correct me if I'm wrong on this George, but what it appears to be, to me, with my total limited understanding, what I appear to be looking at, is half a pint.

(**GEORGE** *clicks his fingers – bingo!*)

(*Beat.*)

Sorry, am I missing something?

GEORGE. What else do you see?

(**ANNA** *begins tapping her foot impatiently.*)

Have another look. Just, you know, properly look at it.

ANNA. OK...

> (**ANNA** *huffs, looks closely at the pint glass.*)

Maybe they didn't want it.

GEORGE. Maybe they didn't want it?

ANNA. Maybe they thought they wanted it when they ordered it, but on closer inspection decided that maybe they didn't want it after all.

GEORGE. Too simple.

ANNA. So why wouldn't they finish it?

GEORGE. That's what I can't quite figure out.

ANNA. Well, when you conclude your imperative investigation, how about you give me a hand in here? Honestly...

> (**ANNA** *shuffles behind the bar and back out with a box of cleaning material.*)

Just stand around, wondering out loud about god knows what. No care about having to be out in the morning, just stand and have a little ponder to yourself, that'll get everything sorted. Leave it to Anna, the cleaning, the sorting, leave it to her. That's woman's work.

GEORGE. What was that?

ANNA. Oh, you know, only me, having a ponder.

> (**GEORGE** *stands in the centre of the room.*)

GEORGE. This look big to you?

ANNA. I know what you're doing you know. You think you're being clever but I know exactly what you're –

GEORGE. Could have fit a snooker table in here, more than enough room to –

ANNA. Honestly George, if you don't start helping me!

(GEORGE trudges over and grabs a rag from the box, starts to wipe the counter slowly. ANNA watches him.)

Tomorrow's going to come whether you move slow or not.

GEORGE. I know. I know. Nobody knows better than me.

(GEORGE picks up another half-drunk pint, feels the weight of the glass in his hands.)

Do you think…it might not be the right thing. Might be a mistake.

ANNA. Might not be. You saw tonight, didn't you? Used to be heaving in here.

I remember Saturdays gone by, it would take me a good twenty minutes to collect people's glasses, that's if no-one came back with theirs for a top up. Twenty minutes across the floor it would take me. You know how long it took me tonight? Under one minute. Tells you everything that does. So no, I don't think it's a mistake at all.

GEORGE. One minute? Bloody hell – how can this be happening? In what world is a pub, the staple of community, the hub of British society, in what world is that no longer where people want to be? How are people going to cope?

ANNA. I tell you who's not coping right now – if you don't bloody help me, you will see what not coping looks like.

(GEORGE walks down the bar, picks up another half drunk pint glass. And another. He assembles a tiny army of nine, not-finished pint glasses.)

You realise that's not helping, don't you? You're just moving the mess around? Please George, I don't ask for much, but please can you help me before –

GEORGE. Nine of them.

ANNA. So, I suppose this is your way of telling me you're not actually going to help pack, is it? Are you going to do anything that needs doing? Clean the lines? Empty drip trays? Pack away the stock?

GEORGE. There's nine of them.

ANNA. Oh I see, so I'm talking to myself now then. Great. Doing everything myself anyway, so what difference does it make –

GEORGE. Nine!

> (**GEORGE** *starts laughing.*)

Country is falling apart at the seams! People start something, they don't finish. Fucking travesty.

ANNA. I've just about had enough of this now. I know what you're doing. You think that if you don't do what needs doing, tomorrow will never come. Well, got news for you sunshine, tomorrow is going to come whether you want it to or not, and I for one, am going to be ready. I know it's a struggle for you love, but we have to get this done.

GEORGE. You don't understand –

ANNA. I'm trying to understand –

GEORGE. You've never understood, that's why you don't care about –

ANNA. Of course I care, I'm just not being dramatic about –

GEORGE. Total lack of care –

ANNA. OK then, George, make me understand!

> (**GEORGE** *picks up an empty pint glass.*)

GEORGE. This here, you got no idea how much this means. This is normal, this is tradition. This is what has been happening in this room for five generations. Since eighteen ninety-three! People coming in, good people, ordering a drink, finishing it, and going on with the rest of their business.

ANNA. Right.

(**GEORGE** *picks up a half-drunk pint glass.*)

GEORGE. This. This is...disgusting. This should never happen, no one should ever swan into their local and order a pint, only to leave half of it. Order half a pint, that's fine, no problem at all. But don't start something and not finish it, that's sacrilege! There comes a time when people no longer see through their decisions and they only half commit, and then give up. They don't have the respect enough to finish, and it's a fucking shame.

ANNA. People have *always* left drink in their glasses –

GEORGE. Not with the same regularity that they do now. When I was a boy, this would have been a rare occurrence. Whole pub would have looked at whoever started putting their coat while with golden nectar still in their jar. And as they were walking out, people would mutter under their breath. They'd curse them. People would shake their heads and lament the twisted nature of a poor lost soul.

ANNA. Maybe they have had enough. Just because they don't finish their pint, you know, it's not some personal attack on you –

GEORGE. Course it is. It's all fucked.

ANNA. Yes George, it's all fucked, the whole thing is fucked! Now, if you're finished – will you stop feeling sorry for yourself and help me? How's it going to look if we hand over the keys to a messy pub?

(*Pause.*)

(**GEORGE** *doesn't move.*)

Do something! Please!

(**GEORGE** *pushes all but one of the glasses off the counter.*)

(*Pause.*)

Oh well that's just brilliant, isn't it?

(**GEORGE** *grunts.*)

GEORGE. You said do something –

ANNA. You've finally lost the plot. You going to clean that up then? Or is that going to be left to me and all?

GEORGE. Five generations we've been here. Five! Since eighteen ninety-three, people would walk past and know that it was an O'Driscoll establishment. This has always been an O'Driscoll establishment. That meant something.

(**ANNA** *puts her cleaning cloth down.*)

(**GEORGE** *looks around the room, holding back tears.*)

All that history, and then after tomorrow...

ANNA. You don't know what they're going to do to it.

GEORGE. Probably turn it into some Jungle club or something.

ANNA. Stop being so dramatic.

GEORGE. Lot of history here.

(**GEORGE** *walks out onto the pub floor.*)

This table, seen a lot of action.

ANNA. Has it?

GEORGE. Oh yeah, seen a whole lot of action, surprised it's still standing to be honest.

ANNA. Something you're not telling me George?

GEORGE. Not like that you dirty... I mean, there's been a lot of things occur over it.

> *(**ANNA** shoots him a knowing look, followed by a grunt.)*

Get your mind out of the gutter love. I'm just saying, that this table has seen a lot of history.

> *(**ANNA** crosses her arms, taps her foot.)*

You remember when that bank got robbed down Hammersmith, couple of years back.

ANNA. Yes...

GEORGE. Well when Gerald and Vincent come in the same night with a couple of sacks, what do you think they were doing on this table?

> *(**ANNA** gasps.)*

Yep.

ANNA. Jesus George.

GEORGE. This has seen everything. This is where Bobby Moore sat the week after lifting the world cup. Just there, think of all the musicians we seen come through here. Seems a shame to end with that odd bloke. What's his name? Bowler?

ANNA. *Bowie*, George. Everyone reckons he's going to be a star.

GEORGE. Bloody typical. Just a weird mess of a human, and people reckon he's what's gonna be a star? Anyway... The walls here, they've seen a lot.

*(**GEORGE** looks around, as if an ethereal being has descended.)*

Yes. A people's history exists in here. Just over there, that's where he...

*(**ANNA** stops.)*

*(**GEORGE** stares at a spot by the bar. Starts to cry.)*

*(**ANNA** is frozen.)*

Fuck /

*(**GEORGE** crushes a glass in his hands.)*

*(**ANNA** rushes over and takes the glass from him, starts to dab as his hand.)*

I just want to feel something.

*(**ANNA** stops.)*

ANNA. So, now, you want to feel something?

GEORGE. Don't be like that love.

ANNA. You couldn't even cry for... George, that's not normal.

GEORGE. I know that, I...don't you think I tried?

ANNA. Did you?

GEORGE. Course I...that's what should be happening, and I couldn't even shed a tear for my own...

ANNA. Not a problem for the pub though. No problem blubbering for the pub but for your own little...your little...

*(**ANNA** tries to compose herself.)*

Why would you...how can you stand there and cry when all those months you just...

(**ANNA** *composes herself.*)

To be honest, I'll be happy to see it go.

(*Beat.*)

GEORGE. What did you say?

ANNA. I will. Seriously. I'll be happy to see it go.

GEORGE. That's why you... What? Why?

ANNA. I can't take another day in this fucking shrine George!

(*Pause.*)

GEORGE. Shrine? Hardly call it a shrine love.

ANNA. What would you call it then? Pictures on the wall, favourite songs playing, old football kits hanging... What's that if not a shrine?

GEORGE. Memorial.

ANNA. Oh, George.

GEORGE. It is. It's a memorial.

ANNA. An eternal memorial.

(*Pause.*)

(*They both shift, unsure of how to continue.*)

Things change love. Not for the best. Not for the worst. Just...everything changes. It has to.

(*Pause.*)

It's nice to see you cry.

(**GEORGE** *snorts.*)

It is. It's nice to see you've...you know.

GEORGE. What?

(Beat.)

ANNA. Got a heart.

(Pause.)

(Both shift awkwardly, unsure of what to do next.)

Anyway...right...just...go and clean the lines George.

GEORGE. Yeah. Yeah, alright. Always hated cleaning the lines.

ANNA. Well, savour it this time, because you'll miss it one day. Wash your hand while you're down there too.

*(**GEORGE** nods, leaves.)*

*(**ANNA** resumes wiping down tables. She shakes her head and stops, before tears overcome her.)*

Godsake George, you had to bring him up today, didn't you?

GEORGE. *(Offstage.)* What?

*(**ANNA** quickly composes herself.)*

*(**GEORGE** steps back in.)*

You say something love?

ANNA. No, just...talking to the pub.

*(**GEORGE** begins to empty out the taps while **ANNA** rubs tables again.)*

GEORGE. I *will* miss it you know. The ritual.

*(**ANNA** grunts a response.)*

Funny how the familiarity of something breeds contempt.

ANNA. Yeah. Funny.

> (**GEORGE** *shuts off the taps and leaves.*)

(To herself.) I know... I still feel you in these walls from time to time. I miss you every day. But I can't keep living in this memory filled place anymore. Not with what happened. Not with you still... I'm not leaving you, not like that, but I can't stay here any... God, I must sound like a bloody idiot.

GEORGE. *(Offstage.)* Sorry?

ANNA. Nothing.

> (**GEORGE** *returns.*)

GEORGE. You still talking to the pub?

ANNA. Just saying my goodbyes.

> (**GEORGE** *pulls on the taps, this time a blue liquid comes out. He thinks a moment and stops, putting the taps back up.*)

GEORGE. Why am I making life easier for them who wants to come and take away everything we have?

ANNA. They're not taking anything away.

GEORGE. They are though, when you think about it. They are. They're taking our livelihood, our establishment. Probably take our name if they could.

ANNA. We didn't have to sell –

GEORGE. Didn't have much choice did we? Everyone else is jumping ship and this new lot are coming in with their bloody music and their...told people we was selling up and they understood. Sell up with pride or admit defeat and change and die. We had to, didn't we? It was either that or slowly rot away while others thrived. No thanks.

ANNA. It's the right choice. Come here.

> (**ANNA** *indicates that she wants* **GEORGE**'s *hand. He holds it out, she rummages under the bar and brings out a small first aid kit, begins to wrap his hand in a bandage.*)
>
> (*Pause.*)

GEORGE. What we gonna do? Maybe I could be a postman.

ANNA. Have to get up early for that –

GEORGE. Or the bank, I could work for the bank –

ANNA. Have to be good at counting for that –

GEORGE. Or a market, somewhere. Del says Romford is booming. Maybe there's one down south.

ANNA. You want to work at a market stall? Out in the cold and rain?

> (**GEORGE** *sighs.*)

GEORGE. I don't know how to do anything else, I –

ANNA. You can learn something new.

GEORGE. What if I don't want to learn?

ANNA. Then another pub. I'm sure there's always space for another pub in Purley.

> (**GEORGE**, *scoffs, disgusted.*)

GEORGE. Well I'd...no. Can't do that. Feel like I'm cheating for a start. It wouldn't feel right.

ANNA. A pub's a pub.

GEORGE. A pub is not a pub! A pub is the establishment for the working man.

ANNA. So set up *another* pub –

GEORGE. Not right.

ANNA. Why not?!

GEORGE. Because my family built this pub. Our blood, is stained deep into the foundations, it's in the walls.

ANNA. Nothing changes that George. Your family still would have built the place.

GEORGE. Yeah. But...legacy and all that.

ANNA. You have to be able to pass on...

> *(Pause.)*

> *(**ANNA** huffs and goes back to cleaning.)*

GEORGE. Our blood runs through here.

ANNA. Nothing can change that.

> *(**GEORGE** nods, snorts.)*

> *(He walks over to a wall, removes his bandage and smears his bloody hand on the wall, leaving a red trail.)*

> *(He steps back and admires it.)*

What the bloody hell have you done that for?

GEORGE. Make sure that they know that this building has O'Driscoll blood in it.

ANNA. What do you think the new owners are going to –

GEORGE. I don't give a shit what they say!

> *(**ANNA** sighs.)*

ANNA. Fine. I'll do that as well. I'll just do bloody everything.

> *(**ANNA** continues to clean. She starts to get more manic.)*

GEORGE. Steady on.

(She rushes through as quickly as she can until she stops suddenly. She stares at a spot by the bar, she starts to cry.)

Alright love, I'll clean it off –

ANNA. No, it's not, it's...

(She gulps back tears.)

That's where he took his first steps.

GEORGE. I remember. He was all wobbly weren't he? You kept running up to him in case he fell and I had to stop you. He had to learn how to do things by himself.

ANNA. Nearly fell straight into the stool.

GEORGE. He'd of been alright, he had a good nut on him. Great nut on him our boy.

*(**ANNA** smiles.)*

ANNA. Do you remember... He used to hide under the table when you'd play hide and seek. Be looking at you right in the eyes, and you had to pretend that you couldn't see him so he didn't get upset. I can still see it, you creeping up and looking through him and then he would shuffle out and go "Daddy... Daddy here I am"...

GEORGE. Yeah. Yeah, I remember /

ANNA. His little voice. His first words. I'll never forget the way he said it.

GEORGE. Once he worked out you'd come, couldn't bloody stop could he?

*(**ANNA** smiles, sighs.)*

It's not too late you know. Nothing is finalised, we could always –

ANNA. No, we should –

GEORGE. We don't have to. We could always, you know, people change their minds all the time –

ANNA. No George. We have to –

GEORGE. But there's so many memories, think of everything that's happened here –

ANNA. I am!

> *(Pause.)*

I can't do anything else but think about it everyday, and I can't, I can't, I can't just stay in this, this, this, smothering – I can't do it anymore! I don't want to... There's too many...

> *(**ANNA** cries. **GEORGE** goes to comfort her, she pulls away.)*

I can't live in here anymore where life and death are. There's so much happiness, but it doesn't even come close to the depths of hurt that bathe the walls, George. Yeah, lots has happened, memories have been formed, but so has pain. So much pain. *(Points.)* Just there is where he fell and chipped off both his front teeth because of the bloody carpet, which I begged you to get taken up and you never listened. *(Points.)* There is where he screamed in agony and I had to get on my knees and pick out glass from his feet for hours all because we missed a broken glass the night before. *(Points to the candle.)* There is where he...he... I'll never forget the look on his face. Running about as usual, and he knocked against something and fell over, bashed his head against the table leg, but like you said, he had a good nut on him, so he was OK, I think. But then the ashtray, that big, felt like a tonne heavy ashtray, when that slid off the table and hit him on the... He was looking at me when... I saw the light fade away and our boy was...and every night you light that bloody candle and I have to be reminded of what happened all over again. I can't do it anymore, do you hear me? Yes, you're right, our blood is stained into the place and I just can't cope with that anymore!

(**GEORGE** *moves over to her, goes to hug her –.*)

Don't you get that bloody hand near me!

(**GEORGE** *backs away.*)

I know it's hard for you, but it's fucking hard for me too, and I can't...everyone we know is leaving anyway, so it's not like we're just up and going. It'll be like we're swimming with the tide. And if we stay it's like we have an anchor which is going to drag us down and down and... I can't stay still anymore George. I can't. I need to move, we, need to move forward. We do. We can't just stop living because... We need to move forward and leaving this place and everything that happened... It's a start. I can't just... I can't do *this* anymore.

(**ANNA** *wipes away her tears.*)

GEORGE. Sorry love.

ANNA. There's too many memories George.

GEORGE. Maybe.

ANNA. Everything changes, doesn't it? Doesn't mean that that's a bad thing.

GEORGE. Yeah, maybe you're right.

(*He picks up the final glass, holds it into the light.*)

ANNA. Don't you even think about it.

GEORGE. No, I won't it's just... Just terrible shame that someone left this... Terrible shame.

(**ANNA** *looks at him.*)

*(He puts the pint glass down and gives her
shoulder a squeeze.)*

(They look into each others eyes and smile.)

(They start to clean up silently.)

*(**GEORGE** goes to speak. Stops. He walks over
and takes a picture off the wall. He strokes it.
He looks around the pub floor.)*

He was beautiful our boy. Wasn't he.

*(**ANNA** stops cleaning.)*

ANNA. Yeah. Yeah he was.

*(**GEORGE** looks around at all the pictures.)*

GEORGE. Feels wrong to take these down. Feels like we're...

ANNA. Like we're what?

GEORGE. Forgetting. Erasing it.

ANNA. No. It's more like we're taking the plasters off to let
the skin heal.

*(**GEORGE** thinks a moment, then takes
another picture off the wall. Then another.
One more. And again.)*

*(**ANNA** watches him the whole time.)*

*(**GEORGE** removes the final picture off the
wall. Steps back, shakes his head.)*

GEORGE. Would you look at that?

ANNA. Yeah.

GEORGE. Just a room at the end of the day, isn't it? Just
a room where you trick yourself into thinking that
memories live.

(They look at each other again, share a sigh and resume silently cleaning.)

(The candle flickers. The pint glass is illuminated as the lights fade.)

Scene Two

(The bar is clear, the boxes boarded up, everything is ready to go.)

(The candle is lit.)

(ELMORN JAMES *stands in the middle of the pub. He wears, a sharp, perfectly fitting suit and holds himself with the utmost pride.)*

(CLARENCE *stands close to him. He's tall and gangly, beyond his years. A tiny clone of his father.)*

(Benny Hill's "The Fastest Milkman In The West" plays on the radio.)

ELMORN. Beautiful establishment.

ANNA. Oh. Thank you. We were up all night cleaning.

ELMORN. No need for that.

ANNA. Well, you know. Couldn't hand it over to you in a state.

ELMORN. Appreciate that.

(Pause.)

(ANNA *switches off the radio.)*

ANNA. My husband'll be down in a moment.

ELMORN. No problem.

ANNA. Never was much of a morning person.

ELMORN. I find it is the early bird that catch the worm.

ANNA. Right. Well... I suppose so, yeah.

(ANNA smiles.)

(**ELMORN** *looks around, grunting at the potential.*)

He shouldn't be long.

ELMORN. No rush.

ANNA. Sorry. He, you know, lifetime of working in a pub, not one for early mornings.

ELMORN. Mrs O'Driscoll, your husband can take as much time as he need, I more than happy simply looking around.

ANNA. Right. I'll just...

(**ANNA** *walks to the back door.*)

(*Shouting without shouting.*) George! George!

GEORGE. (*Offstage.*) I'm coming, I'm coming.

(**ANNA** *smiles.*)

ANNA. Sorry about this Mr James.

ELMORN. Not a problem. Call me Elmorn.

ANNA. Elma.

ELMORN. Elmorn.

ANNA. El...more.

ELMORN. Morn.

ANNA. El...morn.

ELMORN. That's good.

ANNA. Right. Names can be tricky.

ELMORN. So I have found.

(*Pause.*)

ANNA. Have you been here long?

ELMORN. Since I arrive.

ANNA. Oh, good, so you know Brixton?

(**ELMORN** *nods, smiles.*)

And what's your name my love.

CLARENCE. Clarence.

ANNA. Oh, an English accent that's...unexpected.

ELMORN. He born here.

(**ANNA** *smiles.*)

(**ELMORN** *looking around settles on the blood stain on the wall.*)

ANNA. Oh, don't worry about that. Can get a bit rambunctious around here at night.

ELMORN. Apparently so.

ANNA. You'll find out for yourself. People, they're great, but you know, everyone has their moments, don't they?

ELMORN. Indeed.

(*Beat.*)

(**ANNA** *smiles.*)

ANNA. George!

(*She smiles again.*)

(**GEORGE** *trudges in.*)

GEORGE. Alright. Let's get this over with.

(**GEORGE** *sees* **ELMORN** *and* **CLARENCE**.)

(*Muffled.*) Bloody typical this is.

ELMORN. I never catch that –

GEORGE. Lovely to meet you, Mr James, yeah?

ANNA. You can call him El-morn.

>   (**ANNA** *looks for confirmation,* **ELMORN** *nods.*
>   *She beams.*)

GEORGE. I'll stick with Mr James, thanks.

ELMORN. Whatever make you most comfortable.

>   (**GEORGE** *snorts.*)

GEORGE. *(Muffled.)* Don't you worry about my comfort
mate.

ELMORN. Sorry?

GEORGE. Thank you for being so accommodating.

ELMORN. No problem.

GEORGE. Lot of people would have asked us to leave
sooner.

ELMORN. Happy to oblige.

GEORGE. Gave us time to get all the bits and bobs together.

ELMORN. I understand.

GEORGE. Gave us that final Saturday. We thought it would
be packed, a big send off but...seems Brixton ain't what
it used to be, eh?

>   *(Beat.)*

So, erm, which part of Jamaica you from then?

ELMORN. Trinidad.

GEORGE. Oh right. Near Kingston that side?

ELMORN. No.

>   *(Pause.)*

(**GEORGE** *rubs his hands together, gestures to* **CLARENCE**.)

GEORGE. Your helper?

(**ANNA** *pokes him.*)

What?

ELMORN. My son.

GEORGE. Big lad. What are you, eighteen, twenty?

CLARENCE. Thirteen.

GEORGE. Thirteen?! Look at the fucking size of him.

(**ANNA** *pokes him again.*)

What you been feeding him, jungle juice?

ANNA. George!

GEORGE. What?

ANNA. I'm so sorry about my husband, it's an emotional time for him.

(**ELMORN** *smiles.*)

(**ANNA** *pokes* **GEORGE** *again, gestures for him to apologise.*)

GEORGE. It's an emotional time.

ELMORN. No problem.

(**GEORGE** *gestures for them to sit down.* **ELMORN** *does,* **CLARENCE** *remains standing.*)

ANNA. Do you want any squash, my love?

CLARENCE. Erm –

ELMORN. He fine. Tanks.

ANNA. OK. Well if you do want any, or some milk or anything. Or some biscuits, we have biscuits.

(**ELMORN** *shakes his head, politely.*)

GEORGE. So you going to be turning this into another one of you lot's rum shacks or –

ANNA. Stop being so rude!

GEORGE. I'm asking questions, it's rude to ask questions now?

(**ANNA** *huffs,* **GEORGE** *rolls his eyes.*)

(**ELMORN** *smiles, unperturbed.*)

Right, erm, well. Yeah, as you can see, everything is, you know, nice and traditional. In working order.

ELMORN. That's good to know.

GEORGE. And er, you know, everyone already knows about it so, getting punters in ain't going to be a bother.

ELMORN. I hope not.

(**ELMORN** *chuckles to himself.*)

(**GEORGE** *eyes him suspiciously.*)

GEORGE. Right, and, you know, probably want to look at getting the licence renewed and that –

ELMORN. That won't be necessary.

GEORGE. Well, it will, if you want to be selling alcohol, you'll need an up to date licence, otherwise, hefty fines, which you wanna avoid, trust me.

ELMORN. I won't be needing to sell alcohol.

(*Pause.*)

GEORGE. What kind of a pub don't sell alcohol? That's just a room full of sad people, that is.

ELMORN. A room full of sad people is exactly who will be benefiting from my work.

   (Beat.)

GEORGE. Right. What is it you said you did again?

ELMORN. I didn't.

GEORGE. So what is it you do?

ELMORN. Undertaker.

GEORGE. Fuck off –

ANNA. George! Child present –

GEORGE. Really?

ELMORN. Not something that I would joke about.

GEORGE. So what you gonna do with...you're joking ain't ya?

ELMORN. You lose me.

GEORGE. You're going to turn the Queen's Head into a...

   (ELMORN *smiles, nods.)*

No fucking way.

ANNA. Jesus Christ, I'm so sorry.

GEORGE. Don't apologise, what you doing that for?

ANNA. Because you're behaving like a complete barbarian.

GEORGE. Why? Because I don't want a beautiful English pub to be turned a fucking –

ANNA. You're making an absolute fool of yourself, and me.

GEORGE. I am not. I'm being honest.

ANNA. Well, there's being honest and being *honest*, isn't there. Sorry about the language love.

   (CLARENCE *shifts uncomfortably.)*

GEORGE. So what's going to happen?

ELMORN. Work start immediately. No time to waste.

GEORGE. What's wrong with Dunmore and Son's down Effra road?

ELMORN. It doesn't serve *certain* needs.

GEORGE. Needs? It's a funeral mate. What more can they need?

ELMORN. People have different tradition.

GEORGE. Oh right, another one of you lot and us lot kind of thing is it?

ANNA. George, I promise you –

GEORGE. No, hang about, I need some answers. This is a pillar of the community this. Everyone comes here to drink. Every family, from all over Brixton, this is where they come. You can't just get rid of that.

ELMORN. I find people need something different.

GEORGE. And you can't get that at Dunmore and Son's?

ELMORN. Not quite.

GEORGE. You can't just –

ELMORN. I can.

GEORGE. Not if I change my mind sunshine.

ANNA. OK, everybody, let's just –

GEORGE. Stop telling me to calm down!

ELMORN. Mr O'Driscoll, I don't see what the problem –

GEORGE. No, you lot never do.

ELMORN. Pardon?

GEORGE. You heard me.

ANNA. George...

ELMORN. I tink maybe you need to calm down.

GEORGE. I'll talk however I want in my pub.

ELMORN. Is not a fight with you I want, you know.

GEORGE. Good, because you wouldn't survive a minute.

ANNA. I'm so sorry –

ELMORN. Mr O'Driscoll –

GEORGE. No, whatever you got to say, why should I, you lot coming here and driving people out, why should I even consider letting my pub –

ELMORN. And who is going to come in here when it is only us?

GEORGE. That a threat?

ELMORN. A question.

> (**GEORGE** *laughs and shakes his head.*)

GEORGE. Bet you're bloody proud ain't ya?

> (**ELMORN** *doesn't respond.*)

Never even tried. We welcomed you with open arms. Come in, the gates are open, and now... Driving out the real people that lived here their entire lives. We've been here for generations. And everything we had, everything we built...never even fucking tried.

ELMORN. Nobody forcing anybody. You have a choice.

GEORGE. What choice? Getting over-run with loud, troublesome...this used to be the working man's utopia. Years gone by, a beautiful little village away from the anarchy of...we had everything. And now you have... our jobs. Our houses. Our home. But that's all...yeah, take a lovely little English pub and turn it into, what? Some Jamaican death shop.

ELMORN. Trinidadian.

GEORGE. It's the same ain't it. Just keep it as it is.

ELMORN. Cyaa do that.

GEORGE. Why?

ELMORN. Don't serve my community the same way it served yours.

> *(Pause.)*

> *(**GEORGE** and **ELMORN** watch each other.)*

> *(**ANNA** and **CLARENCE** shift.)*

> *(**GEORGE** nods his head.)*

GEORGE. There's five generations of tradition in these walls.

ELMORN. The ting with tradition is, over time, they change or get forgotten.

GEORGE. Typical.

> *(**ELMORN** doesn't respond.)*

ANNA. Can you just excuse us a moment?

> *(**ELMORN** steps aside.)*

> *(**ANNA** drags **GEORGE** to a quiet corner.)*

What are you playing at?

GEORGE. Anna, I can't just, I can't…

ANNA. George, we agreed.

GEORGE. They're going to destroy the Queen.

ANNA. That doesn't…all you put in, and your dad, your grandad, everyone, that doesn't change.

GEORGE. I can't just hand it over to… They're going to tear it down and –

ANNA. Start again. Like *we* are.

GEORGE. But love –

ANNA. Listen to me now. We've made up our minds and we are going to do what we're going to do. All of the past, that doesn't change, but that is *in* the past. You can't hold on to it if it's stopping you from living, can you? I know how difficult this is for you, but if you don't pull yourself together right now, so help me George, I don't know what I'm going to do.

GEORGE. You can't be serious? I am not just going to hand the keys over for them to ruin something what has stood here for that long! These lot all coming, destroying history.

ELMORN. History cyaa change –

GEORGE. Is anyone speaking to you –

ANNA. That's enough! Right, this is it now. What's your last name?

GEORGE. What?

ANNA. Last name, what is it?

GEORGE. O'Driscoll.

ANNA. And that was your father's name. And his father's name. All the way back to when this place was built. But where was that name before? Because that doesn't sound local to Brixton does it? That's not a name that's been here for hundreds and hundreds of years is it?

GEORGE. Obviously not, but what's that got to do with anything?

ANNA. And when your family bought the land, that must have come from somewhere, right?

(**GEORGE** *grunts.*)

Well then, my point is that this is what happens. People come and people go, but what they leave behind, and what they take with them doesn't change. This is the way it goes love. We move on, others come in. What's the point in hanging on and waiting to fall when we have the choice to climb away?

> (**GEORGE** *sighs.*)

GEORGE. Fine.

> (**GEORGE** *shakes his head. He trudges over to* **ELMORN** *and roots around in his pocket. He brings out some keys.*)

Here.

> (**GEORGE** *hands over the keys.*)

> (**ELMORN** *takes them from him and clasps them in his hands.*)

ELMORN. Tank you.

ANNA. You're welcome.

> (**GEORGE** *looks at her.*)

> (*She gestures "what?"*)

> (**GEORGE** *looks back at* **ELMORN** *and then to* **CLARENCE.**)

GEORGE. Suppose this will all be yours one day. Lot of responsibility.

CLARENCE. Daddy's going to teach me.

GEORGE. I bet he is. Yeah. That's what dads…

> (*He stops.*)

> (*He looks to* **ELMORN.**)

We had a son.

(ELMORN bows his head.)

Yeah he...well...this was all meant to be for him one day, little dream of mine, be able to pass something on to my boy. I was gonna teach him how to clean lines. Pour the perfect...anyway. I always... Ciaran his name was. Ciaran O'Driscoll. He was going to be be a great man one day. I was going to teach him to...yeah. Erm. What's the point on holding on to a legacy if there's no-one to pass it on to, eh?

(GEORGE looks around to see ANNA holding back tears.)

Suppose things change eh? Everything has to change at some point or another.

(ELMORN offers pursed lips.)

(GEORGE walks to ANNA and rubs her shoulder.)

ANNA. Can't remember the last time you said his name.

GEORGE. Not since...but feels like it needs to be said. Let it be said in this room once last time.

(He indicates to leave with a nod of his head. She agrees.)

Right. Suppose we better?

ANNA. Leave you to get on.

ELMORN. I happy for you to stay and take all the time you need.

GEORGE. Nah, probably better to...like a plaster, rip it off, you know.

(ELMORN offers a smile.)

(GEORGE looks around the room, sighs.)

(**ANNA** *smiles at* **ELMORN**.)

ANNA. Come on love.

GEORGE. I will, yeah, just...

> (**GEORGE** *stands and takes in a big deep breath.*

OK. Let's...

> (**GEORGE** *and* **ANNA** *walk towards the door.*)

> (*They stop.*)

> (**GEORGE** *turns back into the room and takes a final look. He notices the candle. He walks over to it, about to put it out, but he hesitates.* **ELMORN** *looks from him to* **ANNA**, *and realises the significance.*)

ELMORN. Mr O'Driscoll, you can leave that burning, if you'd like.

GEORGE. Kind of like a little reminder this. Lit it everyday. Everyday. If that burned, it felt like a bit of Ciaran... Well, anyway –

ELMORN. I understand.

> (**GEORGE** *offers a small smile of thanks.*)

GEORGE. Take good care of her, yeah? Just make sure she...you know. Take care of her.

ELMORN. Of course.

> (**GEORGE** *and* **ANNA** *take a final look, grab the radio and leave.*)

> (*The door closes behind them.*)

> (*Pause.*)

(**ELMORN** *smiles and looks around.*)

Yes boy. You see this?

CLARENCE. Yes daddy.

ELMORN. This place have plenty potential.

(**ELMORN** *moves over to a corner.*)

I tinking over here, we have the reception.

(*He moves to the back.*)

And back here, the morgue, yes?

(*He looks to* **CLARENCE.**)

And where you are, that's where we put the front desk. (*Pointing out the areas.*) So, so and so. Yes?

CLARENCE. Yes.

ELMORN. Boy, wap'en to you? You don't feel any excitement?

CLARENCE. I do.

ELMORN. Oh-ho. Because you looking real excited.

CLARENCE. What happened to their son?

(*Pause.*)

ELMORN. I don't know.

CLARENCE. Did he...

ELMORN. It sound to me that he did.

CLARENCE. That's sad.

ELMORN. Yes, it's sad. But these tings happen sometimes, you know?

CLARENCE. I know. I like his name.

ELMORN. Ciaran?

CLARENCE. It's a good name.

ELMORN. Yes, a strong name indeed.

CLARENCE. Much better than Clarence.

ELMORN. You find so?

CLARENCE. Yeah, Clarence is for old men.

ELMORN. That's good then because you'll be old longer than you're young.

CLARENCE. How old was Ciaran?

ELMORN. I don't know.

CLARENCE. Was he my age?

ELMORN. I don't think so.

CLARENCE. That's a young name. Maybe he was young. It's sadder if he's young.

ELMORN. Yes, very sad.

CLARENCE. Is that going to happen to –

ELMORN. Don't worry about any of that, bai. Look at you. Strong, big. *Real* Trini man. Nothing going to happen to you.

CLARENCE. OK. How come they want to leave?

ELMORN. That's how things go. People go, others come. Natural selection ent?

> (**CLARENCE** *nods.*)

> (*Beat.*)

Go bring the box from the van for me.

CLARENCE. Which one?

ELMORN. Which one? I know you know what I want and you asking me which one.

*(***ELMORN** *steups.)*

Gwan.

*(***CLARENCE** *walks outside.)*

*(***ELMORN** *claps his hands, sizes up the room.)*

(He laughs to himself.)

*(***CLARENCE** *walks back in carrying a huge box.)*

(He puts it down on the bar.)

*(***ELMORN** *runs his hand over the box.)*

CLARENCE. Daddy.

*(***ELMORN** *grunts.)*

Is this going to be mine one day?

ELMORN. Of course.

CLARENCE. So I have to learn how to be an undertaker?

ELMORN. You don't want to be?

CLARENCE. It's a bit scary.

ELMORN. What's scary about it?

CLARENCE. Death.

ELMORN. Death is a part of life. Everything that starts must end, everything that's here will one day go to somewhere else.

CLARENCE. Where will I go?

ELMORN. Where do you want to go?

CLARENCE. I don't know. Where do you want to go?

ELMORN. I right where I want to be.

CLARENCE. Is that why you left Trinidad?

ELMORN. Part of it. Another part is that the Queen ask me to come.

CLARENCE. She did?

ELMORN. She ask me, and all you aunties and uncles and cousins, she ask all of we personally.

CLARENCE. Wow.

ELMORN. That's right. We all sent for by royal decree.

(**CLARENCE** *shifts awkwardly.*)

Wa'pen?

CLARENCE. What that man was saying earlier. About people coming in. What does that mean?

ELMORN. It mean that people come and people go.

CLARENCE. Which people?

ELMORN. All people. We are all travellers you know. The Carib people, your ancestors, they were travelling people. As were the African people. You come from a travelling people.

CLARENCE. I do?

ELMORN. Of course.

CLARENCE. I thought I came from here?

ELMORN. You do. But your blood doesn't. That come from far away.

(*A beat, then.*)

CLARENCE. Am I English?

ELMORN. You feel English?

(**CLARENCE** *shakes his head.*)

You feel Trini?

CLARENCE. I think so.

ELMORN. Then that's what you is.

CLARENCE. OK.

(**ELMORN** *runs his hands over the box again.*)

ELMORN. You want to see?

CLARENCE. Yeah!

ELMORN. Eh-eh, who you talk to?

CLARENCE. Yes Daddy.

(**ELMORN** *grunts.*)

(*He brings out a small sign.*)

(*It reads "Nine Nights. Est 1971".*)

ELMORN. You like that?

CLARENCE. Yeah.

ELMORN. Yes that's real nice. You know what that mean?

(**CLARENCE** *shakes his head.*)

I going to teach you. I teach you everything that you need to know. Don't be scared.

CLARENCE. OK Daddy.

ELMORN. Yes boy. This mean something real special. This is a place for we.

(*Lights fade to blackout.*)

ACT THREE

(A new, hipster enoteca.)

(Epicurean. Traditionally decorated, vintage inspired. Modern day.)

(Hipster-dimly lit by vintage, low brightness lamps.)

(A candle burns on a pillar.)

Scene One

(Jungle's "Keep Moving" plays from a bluetooth speaker. At some point, the music changes to Jungle's "The Heat.")

(ANGUS stands behind the bar, lines up three wine glasses and pours out some wine while ESME sits with a blindfold on.)

ESME. Is this blindfold necessary?

ANGUS. Hundred percent.

ESME. But you could just take the labels off if you wanted to.

ANGUS. Ah, but then the problem becomes what wine did I just pour.

ESME. I don't think the blindfold is necessary. I'm taking it off.

ANGUS. No! Leave it! Almost done!

> *(ANGUS finishes pouring out the wine.)*

There.

ESME. Come on, I feel like I'm in Guantanamo.

ANGUS. What a glorious life that would be if they had what you're about to have. *(Picking up the first glass.)* Number one. Try.

> *(ESME tries it, letting the wine swill around her mouth. Her lips smack audibly and ostentatiously. And for far too long.)*

Come on!

ESME. Can you not interrupt my process please?

> *(ESME smacks her lips again.)*

ANGUS. Yes, you've been on a wine tasting course, we get it.

ESME. I'm letting the flavours percolate.

ANGUS. Any chance they can percolate quicker?

ESME. I'm trying to get an emotional reaction.

ANGUS. Just tell me how it tastes –

ESME. An emotional reaction is just as important as taste, we want people to come in and form an attachment, create a memory, an evocation of how they felt when –

ANGUS. I'd quite like people to just enjoy the wine. Just taking simple pleasure without over-analysing –

ESME. Please don't diminish my process, you're ruining my feeling.

ANGUS. Fine. Go ahead.

> (*A couple more swills, gushes and lip smacks from* **ESME**.)

ESME. I've made my discovery.

ANGUS. And?

> (*Beat.*)

ESME. Bland.

ANGUS. Bland?

ESME. Quite bland. Dull. Uninspired.

ANGUS. I'm aware of the meaning, thanks. That's all? That was my first choice.

ESME. Well, that says everything, doesn't it. I feel nothing. A wine should move my spirit and disturb my soul, after that glass I feel...

ANGUS. Yes?

ESME. Well, it feels as if my existence hasn't been altered in the slightest after that glass, put it that way.

ANGUS. It's house wine, it's not supposed to be life changing.

ESME. Next.

> (ANGUS *offers the next glass.* ESME *goes through the same ritual while* ANGUS *waits impatiently.*)

Chocolately notes, an oaky flavour that sits above a hint of citrus. It makes me feel warm, comforted.

ANGUS. Great.

ESME. No, not great, the opposite of great. This is not what we want from a house wine.

ANGUS. But you just said –

ESME. What I mean is that it's familiar. Not in a good or bad way. We want something that stands out.

ANGUS. What does that even mean?

ESME. What do you think it means? Honestly this is pointless. Just let me pick which wine will best fit –

ANGUS. No, no – you said, you said that I – look, you've picked everything about this place. You said wine was mine, it was my thing, and I want my thing –

ESME. But you're clearly out of your depth with –

ANGUS. Let me have my one thing, please!

ESME. I mean, I don't see what the big deal –

ANGUS. It's a big deal to me. OK?

> (ESME *sighs. A beat, then.*)

ESME. Sure.

ANGUS. *Thanks.* Last one.

(**ANGUS** *hands it to her, the same ritual occurs.*)

ESME. Now, this, this is...interesting.

ANGUS. I don't know what that means. Is that good or bad or –

ESME. It feels dangerous. Edgy. It feels like I don't love it but it loves me and I like that.

ANGUS. That just sums you up –

ESME. It feels like it's consumed by a man who would sooner rip my clothes off and ravish me right here before asking my name.

ANGUS. Jesus.

ESME. It's perfect.

(*Beat.*)

ANGUS. Perfect?

ESME. It's the perfect wine for what we want. For the vibe we want to cultivate.

ANGUS. Which is sexual assaulty?

ESME. Which is edgy-urban-chic.

ANGUS. Edgy-urban-chic. Cool.

ESME. Where is this wine from?

ANGUS. Guess.

ESME. I would think with that fiery raw passion that sits beneath the notes... Argentina. Or Spain.

ANGUS. Bit stereotypical.

ESME. Is it? I don't think is.

ANGUS. Passionate and creepy?

ESME. Never said creepy, you imagined creepy.

ANGUS. Anyway, nope. One more.

ESME. South Africa.

ANGUS. How do you go from Spain and Argentina, to South Africa?

ESME. I'm right aren't I?

ANGUS. Nope.

ESME. I see. So where is it from then?

ANGUS. Romania.

(*Beat.*)

ESME. Really? How...unexpected...can I take this blindfold off now?

ANGUS. Yep.

(**ESME** *removes the blindfold.*)

So we're going with the Romanian?

ESME. Yeah. It's risky, it's different. Like I said, perfect.

ANGUS. Great. Well that's it then.

ESME. We're done?

ANGUS. House wine was the last thing to decide on.

ESME. Oh my god!

(**ESME** *lets out a little squeal.*)

I can't believe it's actually happening.

ANGUS. All that hard work and we're finally here.

ESME. This is so exciting. I can't believe that tomorrow night we're opening our own enoteca. What a glorious feeling.

ANGUS. People will get it won't they?

ESME. What's not to get?

ANGUS. Well, for a start, until we started planning this, I'd never even heard of the word enoteca.

ESME. That's part of the charm.

ANGUS. Well, hopefully, tomorrow goes well – it's totally sold out now by the way – it goes well and we're a massive success.

ESME. Of course it will go well, this is exactly what the people round here want!

(ESME *leans in and kisses* ANGUS.)

ANGUS. Is that what you want? Someone who... you know... rips off your clothes without even asking.

ESME. Sometimes. Passion is sexy.

ANGUS. I'm passionate.

ESME. Sure you are.

ANGUS. I am! I'm very passionate. Go and put on a top you don't like and I'll rip it right here like the Hulk.

ESME. Defeats the purpose if you're planning to rip the top doesn't it.

ANGUS. I can do it!

(ESME *smiles, kisses him again.* ANGUS *sighs, upset at not being taken seriously.*)

ESME. This is so exciting.

ANGUS. Know what's even more exciting?

ESME. *(Leaning in.)* Tell me.

ANGUS. Your turn to take out the bins.

(ANGUS *produces a full bin bag.* ESME *huffs and exits with it.*)

(**ANGUS** *tries to rip his shirt, fails. Tries again, nothing. He gives up.*)

(**ESME** *returns, huffing.*)

It's not that bad –

ESME. That man is out there again. Loitering.

ANGUS. Again?

ESME. Yes, he's starting to make me very uncomfortable. His energy is too –

ANGUS. Edgy-urban-chic.

ESME. Very funny. Can you go and say something please.

ANGUS. Like what?

ESME. I don't know. What men say in these situations.

ANGUS. What do men say in these situations.

ESME. I don't know, do I?

ANGUS. Neither do I.

ESME. Just something, to you know, make him…

(**ESME** *makes a gesture of "shoo".*)

ANGUS. Shoo?

ESME. Well no, obviously not but…not rude just…onward fair chap or…you know.

ANGUS. Yes M'lady. Have you ever spoken to him?

ESME. Of course not, he just stands there, as if he's waiting.

ANGUS. Waiting for what?

ESME. Just waiting. Loitering. I don't like the loitering, it makes me uncomfortable.

ANGUS. I'm sure he's lovely.

ESME. Can you just –

ANGUS. Look, this will be good for you actually. This is Brixton, he's probably a native – I'll get him in, get his thoughts on the new place. Think of it as community outreach-based market research.

ESME. I don't think that's a good idea.

ANGUS. It'll be fine.

ESME. Angus, please –

ANGUS. Just relax, look.

> (**ANGUS** *opens the door, pops his head out, while* **ESME** *puffs and shakes her head.*)

Hello mate... Hi, how you doing?... Listen do you want to come inside? Just that we've seen you out here a lot and thought you might be curious...yeah, course, come inside. Yeah, please, I insist.

> (**ANGUS** *shoots a smile back inside,* **ESME** *returns it dripping in sarcasm.* **ANGUS** *holds the door open.*)

> (**CLARENCE** *enters, timid and unsure.*)

Come on, come on, it's fine.

> (**CLARENCE** *settles in the middle of the space. He's more frail now, less sure of himself.*)

ESME. *(As if he's stupid, or doesn't speak English.)* How. Are. You?

> (**CLARENCE** *nods, looking around bewildered.*)

ANGUS. It's quite something isn't it. It's inspired by the '60s and '70s, vintage classics.

> (**CLARENCE** *nods again.*)

We, myself and, oh I'm Angus by the way, myself and Esme, my partner, in business and love, we thought that the space was crying out for some subtlety, a nod to the great past.

    (**CLARENCE** *nods once more.*)

    (*Beat.*)

CLARENCE. I used to spend a lot of time in here.

ANGUS. Oh wow, that's great.

ESME. What did it used to be? When we rented it, everything had been gutted, pretty much everything anyway. There were some fridges in the back that were still here, which cost a fortune to remove – was it restaurant or a butchers or –

CLARENCE. Undertakers.

    (*Pause.*)

ANGUS. Seriously?

    (**CLARENCE** *nods.*)

That is so fucking cool!

ESME. So, those fridges were... Oh God. They should have told us that, surely? I was keeping lunch in those fridges while we waiting for them to be removed. Surely that's against health and safety regulations –

ANGUS. You said you spent a lot of time here?

CLARENCE. I knew the owner.

ANGUS. Ah, right.

    (*Pause.*)

Well, I suppose –

CLARENCE. He loved this place. Worked here his whole life. It was everything he knew.

    (*Beat.*)

ESME. What happened to him?

> (**CLARENCE** *doesn't respond.*)

(To **ANGUS**, *whispering.)* I think this might have been a mistake. I'm not sure he's all there.

ANGUS. *(Whispering.)* He's fine. I think he likes it. Must look so different to before.

CLARENCE. He left. He had to leave.

ESME. Oh. Right. That's… I'm sorry.

CLARENCE. His whole life was in these walls.

ANGUS. Would he, I mean, we're having a launch night and it might be nice, for him to come along, if he'd like to of course.

> (**ESME** *shoots him a look.*)

Or, you know, it might not be his vibe.

ESME. *(Whispering.)* Are you having a breakdown? Why would you –

CLARENCE. He used have a son.

> *(A beat.)*

Him and his son, they run this place together. But his son…his son have a child. A little girl. And she was the most beautiful thing the man ever seen. When he looked into her eyes, he told her, whatever needs to be done, he will do it just to see her smile. He was a good man. A proud man…but, maybe he never get the breaks he need. Maybe the climate change too quickly for him…

His son decide to turn against him and…his son decided that he wanted everything and he couldn't have everything while his father was still alive…so he… he do what he have to do.

ANGUS. What do you mean?

CLARENCE. He killed him.

>   *(A beat.)*

ESME. Oh my god.

ANGUS. That's awful.

CLARENCE. But his son never realise that when he killed his father, he killed both of them. Killed that thing inside that made him *him*. I…can I just…for a moment, just…I can still feel him in here. Can feel *both* of them in here…can I just…

>   *(**ANGUS** and **ESME** exchange looks while **CLARENCE** takes it all in.)*

ANGUS. Yeah. Yeah, that's not a problem. Do you want a cup of tea or anything?

>   *(**CLARENCE** doesn't respond.)*

I'll make you a cup of tea.

>   *(**ANGUS** and **ESME** go to leave, **ESME** points to the door. **ANGUS** creeps over and locks it, before offering an enormous smile to **CLARENCE**.)*

>   *(**CLARENCE** barely registers. **ANGUS** and **ESME** exit.)*

>   *(**CLARENCE** looks around the space, lost. He looks to his hands, tuning them over in front of him. He searches for something of himself in the room.)*

>   *(He looks to the picture of where **ELMORN** used to hang.)*

(His breath starts to quicken, it's all too much.)

CLARENCE.   Daddy... I know you're still here... You see what they done to the place? It's like they take some water and wash away everything about we. You see this Daddy? You tell me this is a place for we. Where do we go now? Daddy? Give me something, tell me where –

> *(He spots the candle against the pillar. He stares at it. His lips might curl into a barely discernible smile, they might quiver.)*
>
> *(The lights slowly fade, until it's just* CLARENCE *and the flickering candle.)*
>
> *(Blackout.)*

End

Lightning Source UK Ltd.
Milton Keynes UK
UKHW020959011021
391486UK00007B/336

9 780573 132742